FINDING COURAGE

FINDING COURAGE

History's Young Heroes and Their Amazing Deeds

by J. M. Bedell

Published by
Beyond Words Publishing, Inc.
20827 NW Cornell Road, Suite 500
Hillsboro, Oregon 97124
503-531-8700

Editors: Barbara Leese, Kristin Hilton, Summer Steele
Proofreader: Jade Chan
Interior Design: Barbara Leese

ISBN: 1-58270-110-5

Printed in the United States of America
Distributed to the book trade by Publishers Group West

Library of Congress Cataloging-in-Publication Data
Bedell, J. M. (Jane M.)
Finding courage: history's young heroes and their amazing deeds / written by J. M. Bedell.
p. cm.
ISBN 1-58270-110-5
1. Children—Biography—Juvenile literature. 2. Heroes—Biography—Juvenile literature. 3. Courage in children—Juvenile literature. I. Title.

CT107.B43 2004
920'.0083—dc22

2003027968

The corporate mission of Beyond Words Publishing, Inc:
Inspire to Integrity

To my heroes:
Donna Gorrell, for being an amazing teacher, and
Nick and Aubrey Olson, who daily live heroic lives.
You inspire me!—JMB

Photo Credits:

Every effort was made to contact the copyright owners of the photographs in this book. If we have not contacted a copyright holder, please inform Beyond Words Publishing. The publisher gratefully acknowledges and thanks the following individuals and organizations for their generous assistance and permission to use these photos:

Manjiro Nakahama: The Yomiuri Shimbun
Louis Braille: JAARS Museum of the Alphabet (http://www.jaars.org)
Iqbal Masih: Broad Meadows Middle School: Kids' Campaign: School for Iqbal (http://www.mirrorimage.com/iqbal/)
Kodjo Djissenou: The Reebok International Human Rights Award Program (http://www.hri.ca/hraward/)
Levi Coffin: Levi Coffin House Assoc. and Waynet (http://www.waynet.org/nonprofit/coffin.htm)
Mary Beth Tinker
Trevor Ferrell
Arn Chorn-Pond
Leonora Shiroka: My Hero Project (http://www.myhero.com)
Ibrahim (Alex) Bangura: My Hero Project (http://www.myhero.com)
Mayerly Sanchez: Daniel Paez (http://www.visionmundialcolombia.org.co)
Alexandra Scott: Alex's Lemonade Stand (http://www.alexslemonade.com)

Contents

Author's note: The people whose stories are featured in this book were chosen for their heroism and bravery. Some of their stories were not recorded until many years after their deeds, and, in some cases, important information was lost. Available accounts of their lives have been studied to make sure that all information included in this book is true; however, some details have been added to account for missing information. To make each person's story come alive, fictional scenes based on historical events begin each chapter.

Introduction

"To reach real peace in the world, we will have to begin with the children."
—Mohandas Gandhi

What is it like to stand face-to-face with an invading army or an angry, screaming mob? Would you risk your own life to stand up for a cause you believed in? Leading a nation in battle, rescuing a fallen friend, feeding the homeless, or crying out for peace—these are the actions of heroes. Have you ever wondered if there is a hero in you?

In this book, you will read the true stories of amazing young heroes—ordinary kids, just like you, who faced extraordinary situations. With courage and determination, they overcame fear and doubt and chose to stand up and fight, to survive, to live. You will meet kids like Sybil Ludington and Pierre Labiche, who understood that freedom is bought with a price and that the price might be their own lives. You'll come to know kids like Susie (Baker) King Taylor and Ryan White, who struggled in a world gone crazy and managed to make life better for themselves and others. You'll also read about Claudette Colvin and Iqbal Masih, whose courage ripped open our eyes to the injustices lurking in our own backyards.

There are courageous kids on every continent and in every nation. From ancient China to modern war-torn Israel, they fought and continue to fight for peace in their homelands, justice for themselves and others, and the right to live, learn, and grow in a world free from hate and tyranny.

Fa Mu-lan (Before AD 600)

China's Great Warrior

Standing at the top of the hill, Mu-lan's gaze traveled across the valley. The bitter west wind whipped her cheeks and stung her eyes. The rumble of many voices vibrated in the morning air. Thousands of tents dotted the valley and smoke from myriad campfires traced tendrils into an azure sky. The great Yellow River silently snaked its way across the land and out towards the open sea. At Mu-lan's feet, spread out as far as the eye could see, lay the great throng of the emperor's mighty army.

Young Mu-lan watched the bustle of activity and her heart raced with fear. Could she really do this?

Knowing that she had little choice, she straightened her back, drew in a deep breath, and whispered to her stallion, "From this moment on, I am no longer a girl. I am a warrior!"

Fa Mu-lan was born in Shang Yau, China, sometime between the third and sixth centuries, in a time known as the Era of Disunity. The daughter of a respectable family, Mu-lan spent her days as many Chinese girls did, preparing meals, washing clothes, and weaving on her loom. Expected to marry and raise a family, girls in ancient China seldom received any formal education, like reading and writing. Instead, they learned important household skills.

One day as young Mu-lan sat weaving, she heard a messenger's cry filter into the room. Twelve times he cried out the news that brutal Tartar tribes had invaded China and that all men must come and fight, according to the emperor's command. Although the message was troubling, it was not unexpected—China was in constant threat of invasion from the Tartars, nomadic tribes that roamed the northern lands known today as Mongolia and Manchuria. The Tartars terrorized the Chinese countryside, plundering fields and raiding cities and towns. They murdered farmers, stole livestock, and looted every home.

China was a huge country with a vast border to protect. In many regions, feudal lords built walls to keep out invaders. In about the third century BC, the walls were joined to form the Great Wall, which stretched across thousands of miles along the northern frontier and ended at the Yellow Sea. At the time that Mu-lan lived, Tartar tribes began invading China, breaking though the Great Wall and raiding farms and villages. This continuous threat forced the Chinese military to seek huge numbers of soldiers to defend the country.

When the emperor's messenger finished his call, he posted the list of names of those who must immediately report for duty. Mu-lan scanned the list and saw her father's name on it, but he was old and frail and Mu-lan was sure that he would not be able to survive the battle. Unfortunately, the order was clear: one man from every house must serve in the emperor's army.

Mu-lan ran to her father's side and begged him not to go. As she comforted him, she struggled to think of a solution. Since there were no sons in the family, someone else must go instead. Mu-lan quickly decided that she would disguise herself as a man and take her father's place in the army.

Her parents strongly protested. A woman disguising herself as a man to fight in battle was unheard of! If anyone found out, the family would be disgraced and Mu-lan would possibly be imprisoned or sentenced to death. But the emperor's word was law: someone from Mu-lan's family must report for battle. For Mu-lan and her parents there appeared to be no other choice.

The notice demanded that the soldiers report by dawn, so Mu-lan quickly formed her plan. To keep her preparations a secret from her fellow villagers, she traveled to different towns to buy a beautiful, powerful stallion, a saddle, a bridle, and a whip.

After returning home with her purchases, Mu-lan prepared her disguise. Her parents watched sadly as she cut her silky black hair and as she marched back and forth across the room, practicing a soldier's gait. As she talked, she slowly deepened her voice so that she would sound more like a man. She put on her father's armor, which was made of stone squares held together by metal clasps; then she assembled his sword, axe, bow, and arrows. The transformation was complete. Before their eyes, their daughter had changed from a beautiful, young girl into a brave, young warrior.

Darkness cloaked the village when Mu-lan crept out of the house and into the stable. She saddled her horse and rode silently through the sleeping village. Once outside the village, she spurred her horse into a gallop and raced towards the Yellow River Valley.

She finally stopped to rest at the rise above the valley. Below her, camped in the snow, was the emperor's ten thousand-man army. Gathering her courage and knowing that her family was depending on her, she kicked her horse's flank and clung to him as he galloped down the hill. Mu-lan reported for duty and settled into camp.

At dawn the army marched north to join the other Chinese armies gathering for war. Their numbers swelled and soon Mu-lan was buried in a sea of soldiers. They would all be needed to battle against the invading Tartars.

The Tartars were a feared enemy force that used its mobility to military advantage, appearing when least expected and surrounding Chinese troops. Known as excellent horsemen, the Tartars bred wild horses into mounts of great strength and stamina. With the invention of the stirrup, their archers soon learned to shoot while on horseback, giving them an even greater advantage.

Mu-lan faced this formidable fighting force on her first morning of battle. The pounding of war drums vibrated in the air as Mu-lan's horse neighed with anticipation, nostrils flaring. The order to attack sounded down the line and the horses surged forward. A mass of horseflesh and armor surrounded Mu-lan, as well as screams of rage and pain. Arrows flew across the sky and soon her thoughts were only on survival and battling the enemy.

Suddenly China's great army began to weaken. Watching the Tartar assault gather strength, many of the Chinese soldiers thought that the battle was lost, but Mu-lan mustered her courage and refused to surrender. She called for them to follow her and for them to be brave and to fight for their families, for their homes, and for China!

The soldiers turned and followed Mu-lan back into battle. The force of their sudden assault surprised the enemy and the Tartar line broke. The Chinese army scattered the Tartars and they fled the battlefield. By nightfall every soldier was telling the story of Mu-lan's courageous attack.

As the months passed, Mu-lan's physical strength increased and she learned to wield a sword with great accuracy. She studied the war strategies of great generals and read the writings of Sun Tzu, the ancient master of warfare. Sun Tzu's book, *The Art of War*, taught her how to plan attacks and position the troops. Her courage, leadership, and tactical skills soon caught the attention of the emperor's officials. She rose through the army ranks and eventually commanded her own company. She even led a small troop that made surprise raids on the Tartars. Finally, after winning hundreds of battles against the Tartars, Mu-lan was promoted to general.

After twelve long years, the war finally ended and Mu-lan was free to go home. The story of Mu-lan's bravery spread throughout the country, and she was summoned to appear before the emperor. She traveled to the royal city of Loyang. An older and wiser Mu-lan entered the palace and bowed before the emperor of China.

In return for her bravery, the emperor offered Mu-lan great gifts: twelve medals of honor and one thousand strings of coins. When asked what other gifts she wanted, Mu-lan simply asked for permission to return home.

Surrounded by an honor guard of soldiers, Mu-lan arrived at her village a few days later. She entered the gates of her home and was greeted with cheers from her family and friends. As the preparations for her welcome feast began, Mu-lan entered the house, happy to be back in her childhood home. She took off her helmet and armor and put on traditional women's clothing. After powdering her face, she combed her hair and adorned it with flowers. When she stepped into the courtyard, her fellow soldiers stared in amazement. They recognized her, but they had had no idea that the brave man they had fought beside for all those years was really a young woman.

One soldier, a special friend whose life she had saved many times, stepped forward and asked her to be his wife. An excited Mu-lan said yes, but under one condition. She asked only that he treat her as an equal, with the same honor and respect as he had when he thought that she was a man. He happily complied.

Today children of China are still told this heroic story. Fa Mu-lan is remembered in poems, ballads, and Chinese opera. A temple in Yin Kok village silently protects the ancient stone tablets that tell the story of this great warrior. It honors the memory of the young girl who went into battle and helped save a nation.

King Alfonso XI, "The Avenger" (1311–50)

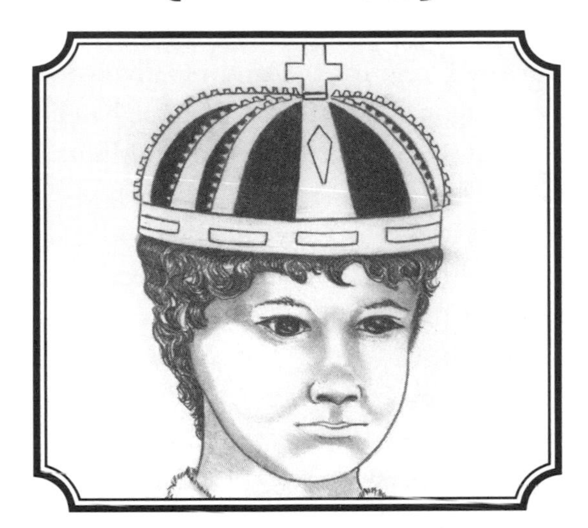

Liberator of Castile-León

The door opened and members of the council slowly filtered into the chamber. Fourteen-year-old King Alfonso stood at the head of the table, his fingertips nervously tapping his right thigh. His advisors moved about the room, speaking to each other in hushed tones. Alfonso knew that they were asking why a special meeting had been called.

After the last man passed through the heavy wooden doors, the guards pulled them tightly closed. Each advisor took his seat at the round table as Alfonso handed an official document to the council's leader. When all were seated, Alfonso said, "I have decided to end my minority. I am now old enough to manage the affairs of my kingdom. The regents have fulfilled their duty. From this day forward, I will rule Castile-León!"

Never before in the history of Castile-León had a king so young taken matters into his own hands and come to such a decision. Alfonso knew that his people were suffering, but could he save them? Was he strong enough to stand up to the powerful regents?

When Alfonso entered the world on August 13, 1311, in Salamanca, he was the undisputed heir to the throne of Castile-León, a kingdom carved from lands that once belonged to Muslim Moors who invaded and conquered what is known today as the Iberian Peninsula. The people wondered what the future held for this royal son whose fate was to inherit a kingdom torn apart by internal strife.

In the early fourteenth century, the land was divided into five kingdoms. Castile-León, Aragon, Navarre, and Portugal had been reclaimed by Christians, but Granada was still ruled by Muslim Moors. The kingdoms had never obtained any lasting peace. There were treaties and alliances, but the shadow of war often settled over the region.

Alfonso's father, Ferdinand IV, "The Summoned," ascended to the throne when he was only nine. He married Constancia, daughter of King Denis of Portugal, when he was fifteen and she was eleven. The alliance ended a war between their two countries. A weak leader, King Ferdinand was unable to control the power-hungry nobles in his own country. When Ferdinand suddenly died on September 9, 1312, while planning a raid on Granada, he left his one-year-old son a kingdom in chaos.

Alfonso was too young to accept his throne. His mother became regent so that she could officially govern until he was old enough to rule the kingdom on his own. Unfortunately, she died a year later.

Regency was then given to two of Alfonso's uncles and his grandmother, dowager Queen Maria de Molina. Following the sudden deaths of Alfonso's two uncles, the dowager queen bravely maintained control over the kingdom's nobility. For the next two years, Alfonso and his sister, Leonor, lived in the town of Valladolid and were educated there. When the dowager queen died in 1321, eleven-year-old Alfonso lost the one family member who genuinely wanted what was best for the young king.

After a bitter royal struggle, the regency went to another uncle, Felipe; a cousin named Juan "el Tuerto"; and Don Juan Manuel. Before long, the three regents began systematically dividing Alfonso's kingdom into three regions. They soon became dissatisfied with what they had and began to fight amongst themselves. Since none of the regents trusted the others, their internal battles caused widespread disorder and then outright lawlessness. Factions in each region began battling each other and brutally killing those who opposed them. Fearing for their lives, many people fled to neighboring countries like Portugal and Aragon. For those who stayed, whether loyal to the king or just wanting an end to the violence, young King Alfonso was their only hope.

In August 1325, after four years of chaos, an angry Alfonso decided to take matters into his own hands. Even though he was only fourteen, he would end his minority and put a stop to the regents' abuse of power. Mustering all his courage, he sent a message to the warring regents, commanding them to stop fighting. Then he called for a meeting of the cortes at Valladolid. The cortes was a group of nobles from across the land, who, when summoned by the king, made important decisions regarding the kingdom's welfare.

At the meeting, Alfonso stood face-to-face with the three most powerful men in his kingdom who had controlled every aspect of his life. To everyone's amazement, he declared that he was old enough to take control of the kingdom's affairs and asked that the regents surrender their authority. His announcement angered the regents, but Alfonso stood resolute. He had wisely armed himself with a previously arranged alliance with his now ex-regent uncle Felipe. With that alliance, he deftly avoided any possibility of the three regents aligning against him. In September 1325 the regents relinquished their authority to Alfonso.

For any king in medieval times, the territories he conquered and colonized and the laws he established were a measure of the success of his reign. Alfonso knew that his ancestors had failed in these areas, but he was determined to succeed. First he would need to rid his country of the men who were destroying it. Then, to curb the flow of refugees to other countries, he would have to convince his people that it was safe to remain in Castile-León. After that, he could focus on conquering other lands.

Alfonso quickly proved that he was more than prepared to rule his kingdom. After dismissing his regents, he turned his attention towards winning over the nobility. No king could reign effectively without its support. Although it took several years of open conflict, Alfonso's leadership and diplomatic skills secured enough support so that the nobles never rebelled during the remaining twenty-five years of his reign.

Alfonso now had time to focus on reclaiming Granada. Although Castile-León was officially a Christian kingdom and openly hostile to the Muslim kingdom of Granada, Alfonso knew that many of his people had social and political systems based on Muslim traditions. It was up to him to find a way to bridge the gap between his Muslim and Christian subjects. He needed to establish laws that would be fair to all groups.

Earlier kings had been unsuccessful in their attempts to impose a universal Christian code of law. Alfonso knew that a king's authority was supposed to be absolute, but he felt strongly that each territory's customs and laws should be respected, whether they were Christian or Muslim. Alfonso's decision to establish laws that respected both religious traditions further helped to unify the country.

Soon after Alfonso's marriage at age seventeen to Dona Maria of Portugal, he established his own knighthood called the Order of the Band. His knights wore white clothes with a black band across their chests. Similar to the famous Three Musketeers, they swore allegiance to the king and promised to uphold the ordinances of chivalry that governed the way they behaved in battle and towards each other.

With his kingdom secure and his wife expecting their first child, Alfonso decided to finish what he had started at Valladolid when he was fourteen. It was time to be dubbed a knight and officially crowned king of Castile-León. A royal coronation was a rare event. Usually each king simply succeeded to the throne upon the death of his successor. But on July 25, 1332, twenty-one-year-old Alfonso crowned himself and then his queen at a ceremony in the city of Burgos. The official coronation was followed by weeks of festivals, feasts, and jousting tournaments.

During Alfonso's reign he increased the territory of his kingdom, built a massive fleet of ships, and formed alliances with neighboring nations. By reducing the powers of the nobility, he helped protect his people from the possibility of future abuse. He helped the landless peasants by easing the terms of their farming contracts. He began to change the justice system by establishing laws that were consistent throughout the kingdom. And he organized an official treasury to stabilize the kingdom's finances.

The courage and strength of the young king of Castile-León brought order to a troubled region. Alfonso XI was the most capable king in Castilian history, but he is perhaps the least known. He ruled over his kingdom until March 27, 1350, when he died of the Black Plague while overseeing the Battle of Gibraltar.

Tom Savage (1594–1627)

Interpreter and Peacemaker

Excited whispers penetrated the darkness and woke Tom. Through the smoky haze from a cooking fire, he saw a messenger speaking with frantic gestures to Chief Powhatan. Fifteen-year-old Tom felt the chief's intense gaze on him and kept his eyes closed, faking sleep. As he listened intently, he heard the messenger tell Chief Powhatan that the Jamestown colony's leader, Captain John Smith, was dead.

Trying to control his breathing, Tom realized that his life and the lives of the colonists were in danger. If Captain Smith was truly dead, then Chief Powhatan would assume that the colony was weak and vulnerable to attack. Then Tom heard what he had feared most: Chief Powhatan ordering his people to prepare for war.

After the chief and his warriors left, Tom slipped out from under his fur cover. He crept silently through the shadows and out into the night. When he reached the edge of the village, he ran, fearing that the warriors might reach the colony before he could warn his friends. Tom ran all night, across streams and through tangled underbrush, hoping to reach the colony in time.

Tom Savage was born around 1594 in rural Chester, England. Some scholars say he was an orphan; others say he was a runaway. Tom had an adventurous spirit and a determination to see the world. At the age of thirteen, he convinced Captain Christopher Newport to take him aboard his ship as his cabin boy and indentured servant. Tom sold seven years of his labor in exchange for food, shelter, and travel expenses to the New World.

On an October day in 1607, Tom boarded the *John and Francis*, a ship filled with settlers, sailors, and soldiers, and embarked on a perilous adventure across the vast ocean. He knew that life aboard the small ship was dangerous. Storms could tear it apart, sickness often wiped out entire crews, and fire could quickly consume a vessel and send it to the bottom of the sea.

Three months later, Tom arrived in the Jamestown colony, located in what is now the state of Virginia. Jubilant colonists greeted the arrival of the ship and its lifesaving cargo of food. The crew was shocked to learn that clashes with the Indians and the search for gold had kept the settlers from planting sufficient crops and storing enough food for the winter. Of the original 105 settlers, only thirty-eight remained, and many were starving or diseased. To make matters worse, only a few days after Tom's arrival, a devastating fire destroyed the struggling colony's valuable food supplies.

Tom wanted to help. He sailed with the colony's leader, Captain John Smith, and Captain Newport up the York River to Werowocomoco, the home of the Native leader, Chief Powhatan. They went on an official visit, hoping to trade for corn and somehow gain Chief Powhatan's trust.

Chief Powhatan was an absolute ruler, so powerful that Captain John Smith said that "even [his] frown caused people to tremble."[1] When Chief Powhatan first came to power, he built a confederacy of more than thirty tribes in the Virginia Tidewater region. The confederacy included the Arrohateck, Appamatuck, Mattaponi, Pamunkey, Powhatan, Youghtanund, and many other tribes. It was important to the colony that the relationship between the two societies remain civil.

During the voyage up the York River, Tom learned that Captain Smith intended to offer him to Chief Powhatan as a symbol of the colonist's goodwill. Smith explained that Tom was to live with the Powhatan tribe, learn its language, and report any plans for an attack on the colony. In exchange, Smith hoped that Chief Powhatan would offer him a young brave whom he would then send to England as a firsthand witness of the powerful country that supported the colony.

Since Tom was an indentured servant, he had little say in his fate but was promised an early release from his contract if he cooperated. The adventurous Tom was willing to make the exchange. Since Smith and Newport knew that Chief Powhatan would not accept a mere servant for such an important exchange, they decided to lie about Tom's identity.

Standing before the powerful chief, Newport falsely explained that he was the ruler of the colony and that Tom was his son. These lies made Tom nervous, and he wondered if he had made a mistake. Powhatan accepted Tom as a token of the colony's friendship and, to Newport and Smith's delight, offered them a young Native boy named Namontack. Once the exchange was complete, tensions between the colonists and the Native tribes calmed.

Young Tom immediately became friends with Powhatan's daughter, Pocahontas. They were the same age, and she introduced him to village life and taught him to speak Algonquian, the tribe's native language. Two of the young boys in the village, Kocoum and Weanock, also became Tom's friends and taught him to hunt. Tom settled into village life but worried because he was there under false pretenses. If Powhatan learned that Tom was merely a servant, he might have him killed.

Tom's life became even more endangered when word reached the colony that Namontack had been killed during a fight aboard the ship taking him to England. If Powhatan found out, he might kill Tom to avenge Namontack. As time passed, with no word to the tribe about Namontack's fate, Tom's secrets became harder and harder to hide.

While Tom lived with the Powhatan, relations between the colonists and the tribes began to deteriorate. As more and more people arrived from England, other settlements encroached on Native American lands. The tribes fought back for their territory, and the atmosphere of distrust soon led to open hostility.

In May 1608 Powhatan sent fourteen-year-old Tom to Jamestown to demand the release of several captured Native people. Tom tried to persuade the colonists to negotiate the release but returned to Werowocomoco empty-handed. Angered by Tom's failure, Powhatan expelled him from the village. A short time later, Pocahontas appeared at the gates of Jamestown, begging Tom to return to the tribe and declaring that her father loved him and wanted him back.

Tom returned and remained with Powhatan until one night in October 1609 when a messenger arrived with news that Captain Smith was dead. With the military leader gone, Powhatan saw his chance to fight back and protect his people and land from the encroaching settlements. Powhatan knew that the colony was vulnerable. He ordered his warriors to prepare for battle. Tom knew that he must warn the colony.

With Powhatan busy with war preparations, fifteen-year-old Tom slipped into the night, trekking through the forest and reaching the colony at dawn. The guard on duty mistook him for a Native and aimed his musket. Tom called out in English and identified himself. Once inside the compound, he learned that Captain Smith had not died but had suffered serious gunpowder burns and had returned to England to recuperate. Tom warned the colony's leaders of Powhatan's plans to attack and helped rouse the settlement. Frantic preparations began as Tom waited for the tribe's warriors to arrive.

The settlers were greatly outnumbered. Every man who had a gun stationed himself along the wall of the fort. Even the colony's English prisoners were set free to help fight. This was a battle for the survival of the settlement.

The woods around Jamestown soon filled with Native warriors. As morning light filtered through the clouds, they scurried through the brush, hid behind fallen trees, and assumed battle positions. Tom crouched low as the first arrows soared across the sky. English muskets fired into the forest, and soon the air was filled with puffs of smoke.

Arrows were no match for muskets and cannons, and eventually the Native warriors were forced to retreat into the woods; however, there was little cause for celebration inside the colony's protective walls. The warriors set up camp in the forest and kept the settlement under siege. For months the colonists were unable to hunt or carry fresh water from the springs. Food became scarce and the water supply turned rancid.

In desperation Tom prepared to return to Chief Powhatan. He would carry a message from the Jamestown officials, a plea to negotiate an end to the siege. He knew that Powhatan would be angry and could possibly kill him for revealing the tribe's plans. After passing through Native territory, Tom arrived safely at Werowocomoco. He was taken before Chief Powhatan, who spared his life and listened to the colonists' plea. Chief Powhatan refused to call off the siege, forcing Tom to spend the winter with him. For months Tom desperately tried to convince the chief to free the colony.

Back at the colony, food supplies dwindled. The winter of 1609–1610 would later be known as the Starving Time. Cold weather, lack of food and water, and disease decimated the village, but at least Tom was able to persuade Chief Powhatan to keep his warriors from attacking. This undoubtedly saved the lives of some of the colonists.

After surviving the devastating winter and being reinforced by ships arriving from England with supplies and additional soldiers, the colonists continued their conflict with the Native tribes. Tom often traveled between Jamestown and Werowocomoco, trying to find a way to bring peace to the region. But neither side was willing to compromise.

Tom served the time of his indenture, but once free he continued to live a dangerous life. He moved between the two cultures but couldn't show favoritism to either one. The colonists valued Tom for his negotiation skills but didn't trust him, knowing that he was close to the people in the Powhatan tribe. The Native people valued him for his language skills but also didn't trust him, fearing that he would reveal their plans to fight the colonists.

Some tribal warriors disliked Tom so much that they taunted the colonists with this war chant: "*Mattanerew shashewaw erowango pechecoma Thom. Newport inoshashaw neir in hoc nantion monocock*," which meant that they would do their best to wound or kill the interpreter.[2] Tom's valued skills were probably all that kept him alive during this time.

In late 1613 Pocahontas was kidnapped by Captain Samuel Argall, a member of the Jamestown colony. Argall offered to release Pocahontas if Powhatan returned several English colonists he had taken prisoner and paid a ransom. Powhatan refused and Pocahontas remained with the colony. She was eventually released but, with Powhatan's consent, returned to marry a tobacco farmer named John Rolf.

Pocahontas's marriage paved the way for peace between Powhatan and the colonists. Nineteen-year-old Tom negotiated the truce that ended the Anglo-Powhatan War and helped restore harmony between the two warring groups.

In 1614 Tom joined a goodwill delegation to Werowocomoco. The peace treaty and Pocahontas's marriage to an English settler allowed Powhatan and Tom to forgive past grievances.

Peace was enjoyed until October 1621, when Tom discovered that the Opechancanough tribe planned to launch an attack on the colonies. This time, Tom tried to warn the new governor of Jamestown, Sir

Francis Wyatt, but was ignored.

On Friday, March 22, 1622, warriors attacked settlements up and down the James River. One-fourth of the colonial population—330 men, women, and children—died in the Powhatan Uprising. The devastated survivors on both sides turned to Tom and another interpreter named Henry Spelman as their last hope. With time and dedication, Tom and Henry renewed the colony's relationship with the Indians. Throughout the second Anglo-Powhatan War (1622–32), Tom negotiated alliances with various tribes. He was also instrumental in procuring much-needed corn and land for settlement, as well as establishing a robust fur trade.

Tom Savage was declared the official interpreter for the colonies. In 1624 he married a woman named Hannah and they settled down on a 150-acre plantation on the eastern shore of Virginia, which is known today as Savage Neck. Tom also held the title to a nine thousand-acre piece of undeveloped land given to him by Chief Powhatan's successor, Chief Debeavon, the "Laughing King." When he died in 1627 at the age of thirty-three, Tom had spent most of his life trying to keep peace in the region.

"It is well past time to take a second look, giving credit for the founding of the [Jamestown] colony where such credit is also due . . . to men like Savage, who devoted their lives to the venture." [3] —Martha Bennett-Stiles

Sybil Ludington (1761–1839)

Revolutionary War Messenger

A crack of thunder shook the house and lightning illuminated the frightened faces of the children sitting near the fire. The pounding of a fist rocked the bolted door. Young Sybil grabbed a musket as her father signaled for the children to hide. She pointed her weapon at the door as her father slowly opened it. A wounded man, soaking wet, staggered in and slumped onto the floor. Her father immediately recognized the man as a messenger and helped him to his feet.

Within moments, the man was sitting near the fire with a blanket covering his shivering body. The look of terror never left his face as he told them how the British had attacked Danbury. They had murdered civilians and torched everything in their path. Sybil watched her father's concern turn to rage. If the British were in Danbury, it wouldn't be long before they invaded the Putnam County countryside, where the family lived.

Someone had to notify the regiment's soldiers, but the wounded messenger could ride no farther. Sixteen-year-old Sybil stepped forward. "I will go," she said.

Sybil Ludington was born into a family known for determination and courage. Her father, a former British officer, had joined the revolutionary cause after resigning his commission in 1775. By the time Sybil was fourteen, much blood had been shed on both sides of the Revolutionary War, and there was little hope of peace.

Known as both a tomboy and an excellent rider, Sybil preferred to watch her father, "The Colonel," train patriot militiamen than help her mother with household chores. Her home was a center of revolutionary activity in a county deeply divided. Even many of her neighbors were loyal to the British.

The Ludington house was a safe haven for one of the revolution's best spies, Enoch Crosby. Crosby's true identity was a closely guarded secret, and Sybil was often included in the discussions of his activities. She knew secret spy codes and secret spots in the house to hide him. Sybil and her sister Rebecca kept watch on the nights their father was away or asleep. They would warn Crosby to stay away if there was any activity in the woods around their house.

Sybil's sentry duty took on added importance after several failed attempts to kill her father. The British had put a price of three hundred English guineas on his head—dead or alive. One night as Sybil stood at the upstairs window staring into the darkness, she spotted movement in the woods. Enemy soldiers quickly surrounded the house. She hurried to wake the other members of her family. After lighting candles and placing one in each window, Sybil grabbed their muskets and handed one to each of the younger children. She told them to march back and forth, pretending to be soldiers. While the children marched, Sybil, her parents, and the older children moved from window to window, trying to make it look like the house was full of men. The ruse worked. The enemy soldiers stayed in the woods. At dawn, after several terrifying hours, they left without attacking or trying to capture Sybil's father.

By April 25, 1777, the night the wounded messenger staggered into the house, Sybil was ready and willing to perform the most dangerous mission of her life. She listened in horror as the messenger told his story: Two thousand British soldiers were drunk and on a rampage. They had murdered civilians, looted buildings, assaulted women and children, and then burned everything in their path. They were fanning out across the countryside and soon would reach Putnam County. Someone had to stop them!

It would take a rider all night to alert the militia. Sybil knew that the ride would be long and dangerous and that the injured messenger would never make it. Her father needed to stay and organize the men when they arrived. And there wasn't even a close neighbor to call on.

Sybil realized that this was her chance to help the revolution. She approached her father and told him that she would ride out and alert the men. At first he hesitated, but Sybil argued that she was an excellent rider, knew the roads, and knew exactly where each soldier lived.

Armed with a musket, Sybil jumped onto her horse and rode into the pouring rain. As she clutched her cloak, she couldn't help but wonder what lay ahead. She might face bands of deserters, bandits, or even the invading British soldiers.

Many of the farms lay in isolated areas where the roads were barely recognizable in the daytime, let alone on a rainy night. Sybil relied on her memory of landmarks to direct her. Huge trees, a large rock, or a bend in the road were often the only signs marking each lane. She rode up to a house, steered her horse near a door, and pounded on it with her musket. She screamed into the night, trying to be heard over the storm, "Danbury is burning! Meet at Colonel Ludington's by daybreak! Bring your arms! The British are coming!"

On and on she rode through the night. House after house, she called out her message and quickly rode on. Within an hour of her departure from their houses, tired men began arriving at the Ludington home, talking about the girl who had summoned them from sleep. The entire regiment was assembled shortly after dawn. After nine hours and over fifty miles, Sybil's ride was finished, and she was trembling with exhaustion. Her father helped her dismount and thanked her for what she had done.

Colonel Ludington's regiment quickly joined forces with five hundred other militiamen and headed towards Danbury. Even though the British outnumbered them, the angry patriots attacked. In one of the first recorded battles using guerilla warfare, the patriots sent the enemy scrambling.

Sybil spent the rest of the war aiding her father in any way she could. Alexander Hamilton praised her heroic ride, and General George Washington made a special trip to her house to meet her. Sybil's courage in a time of crisis was an inspiration to her father, his men, and a new nation.

"Such is the legend of Sybil's ride
To summon the men from the countryside
A true tale, making her title clear
As a lovely feminine Paul Revere." [1]
—"Sybil Ludington's Ride" by Berton Braley

James Forten (1766–1843)

Revolutionary War Hero

Fear enveloped James as the lookout announced that a British ship was on the horizon. The news ripped through the crew of American revolutionaries, and within minutes, the call was heard for all hands on deck. Fifteen-year-old James raced to his station as the ship changed course to prepare for battle.

The first blasts of cannon fire echoed in his ears and the ship rocked beneath his feet. The air filled with the smell of gunpowder and the cries of wounded men. For what seemed like hours, James struggled to keep the cannons supplied with ammunition. The midday sun beat on his head. His back muscles burned. His fingers ached and his legs cried out in protest. Through the pain, James continued to fight.

One by one, the gunners at the cannons crumpled to the ground, either injured or dead. With renewed strength and determination, James continued to supply the cannons and fight against the British ship. Exhausted, he wondered if he would live to see the morning light.

Born on a warm September day in 1766, in a tiny house on the corner of Walnut and Third in Philadelphia, James Forten would soon learn that he was luckier than most. He was born into an African-American family that had obtained freedom, while most other black children in the Colonies were born into slavery.

James's father worked for a sail maker, and James spent his childhood working with his father to learn the trade. At the age of seven, James's father died and the boy's world changed forever. With little time to grieve, his mother turned her attention towards keeping her children fed and educated, and she enrolled James in the Friends' African School; James's practical training at the warehouse ended and his formal schooling began.

A few years later, James heard the Declaration of Independence read to the citizens of Philadelphia. The Colonies declared that they wanted to be free and independent from Great Britain's control. It sparked a fire in James that would never be extinguished. Freedom from Great Britain could mean freedom and equality for all men in the Colonies, black and white.

James's euphoria over the possibility of independence changed into despair when General George Washington suffered one defeat after another in his battles against the British. On the morning of September 26, 1777, British troops marched through Philadelphia. Enemy soldiers controlled the streets, confiscated guns, and occupied people's homes. When the troops finally left the city the following summer, they burned warehouses full of shipbuilding materials and every vessel under construction in the harbor. As James watched flames devastate the wharf, he knew that as soon as he was old enough, he would join the fight against the British.

By the time James turned fifteen, he decided that it was time to join the revolution. As war raged in other parts of the country, Philadelphia emerged as a haven for sea captains intent on attacking and capturing British ships. These men were called privateers. James signed on as a powder boy with the crew of the *Royal Louis*, under the command of Captain Stephen Decatur.

James's first voyage combined the might of the *Royal Louis* with an ally ship, the *Holker*. Together, these ships captured four British vessels. Later they joined several other privateering ships and the number of captured vessels increased. Ships often surrendered without a fight, but one, the British warship *Active*, put up quite a struggle.

Minutes past dawn one morning in August 1781, James experienced the fiercest of sea battles. After hours of fighting, every gunner was dead, but the horror James had felt during the battle changed to triumph when the *Active* finally surrendered. The crew of the *Royal Louis* returned heroes, greeted by cheers from a welcoming crowd. Later James learned that the *Active* carried vital information about a fleet of British ships on its way to the New York harbor, so the *Active's* defeat had proven more important than anyone had thought.

Filled with pride and renewed courage, James signed on for a second voyage. A few days later, with all hands on deck, the lookout spotted a ship on the horizon. Recognizing it as British, Captain Decatur defiantly raised the American revolutionary flag and ordered more sail. For seven hours, the ships chased each other across the open sea. Finally, as cannon-balls hit the water and the *Royal Louis* rocked beneath his feet, James heard Captain Decatur give the order to surrender.

As James boarded the British ship *Amphion*, he realized that the unthinkable had happened: he was a prisoner of war. What he feared most was that the British would send him and the other black crew members to the West Indies and sell them into a life of slavery. Even if he escaped this fate, he knew that he might spend the rest of the war aboard a British prison ship.

A few days later, as the *Amphion* sailed towards New York, James and his fellow prisoners were allowed to play a game of marbles on deck. With one last perfect shot, James's marble tapped his opponent's and James won the game. James's skill caught the attention of the ship's captain, John Brazey, who desperately needed a companion for his younger son, Henry. When the captain realized that James could also read and write, he ordered him to keep Henry occupied.

The *Amphion* dropped anchor near the prison ship *Jersey* and the transfer of prisoners began. In an effort to save the life of his son's new friend, the captain summoned James to his quarters and offered him a chance to sail to England as Henry's companion. He told James that Henry was the heir to a vast estate and could do great things for him. If he accepted, he would eventually return home wealthy and educated.

Here was James's chance. He could escape starvation, disease, possible slavery, or even death, but love for his country and his belief in liberty made it impossible for him to accept the captain's offer. He said, "I have been taken prisoner for the liberties of my country, and never will prove traitor to her interests."[1] The disappointed captain wrote a letter to the commander of the prison ship, asking him to treat James kindly.

James never forgot the compassion offered to him that day, but by nightfall, all he could think about was survival. Aboard the prison ship, James kept close to his fellow shipmates from the *Royal Louis*. They formed a tight-knit group that offered both loyalty and protection. By working together, they had the best chance at surviving the heat, sickness, and hunger that took the lives of other men aboard the ship.

Many times James wished he were on that ship to England, especially when he was pounding bread to dislodge the worms in it, washing the deck, emptying foul-smelling "necessary" buckets, or rowing ashore to help dig graves for the dead. Diseases such as scurvy, yellow fever, and smallpox were rampant aboard the ship.

The prisoners often thought of escape. Unfortunately the waters around the *Jersey* were cold and the closest land was two miles away. If a man managed to sneak overboard and survive the swim to land, he would have to struggle through mudflats and hide in an area heavily occupied by British troops.

So James patiently waited for his opportunity to escape. One day as he sat watching patriot officers being traded for British officers in a mutual prisoner exchange, an idea came to him. At the first opportunity, he approached the next patriot officer on the exchange list and asked if he could hide in his sea chest. The officer agreed.

A few hours before the exchange, James and his friend Daniel went below deck and quietly opened the officer's trunk. They removed several items, allowing only enough room for a body to fit. As he whispered farewell to Daniel and began to climb into the trunk, James suddenly decided that Daniel, his constant friend and fellow Philadelphian, should be the one to survive. He climbed out and told Daniel to take his place. Knowing that he was risking his life, James helped carry the old chest down the ramp and watched with satisfaction as the trunk was carried off the ship. James had sacrificed his own freedom for Daniel's and in return made a lifelong friend.

Victory in the War for Independence came with the signing of the last peace treaty on September 3, 1783. After surviving seven months in captivity, James was finally released. He walked barefoot for more than sixty miles across New York to Trenton, New Jersey. Thin and weary from his ordeals, James arrived at his mother's house and fell into her loving arms. It took months for him to regain his physical health.

James was bitterly disappointed to discover that America's hard-earned freedom did not extend to all its people. The right to citizenship in the new country of the United States of America would not be granted to black people. Still determined to make a place for himself in the world, young James focused on building a career in the sail-making industry. He quickly gained a reputation as an astute and fair businessman.

James delayed marriage because of financial obligations to his mother, Margaret, and his poor sister, Abigail, her husband, William Dunbar, and their four children. Finally, at the age of thirty-seven, he married twenty-year-old Martha "Patty" Beatte. Sadly, Patty died only seven months later.

Soon afterwards, James's brother-in-law also died, and James's responsibilities towards his sister and her children increased. Despite the burden, he married again on December 10, 1805. The bride was twenty-year-old Charlotte Vandine, who bore James nine children: four sons, James Jr., Robert, Thomas, and William, and five daughters, Margaretta, Charlotte, Harriet, Sarah Louisa, and Mary Isabella. Despite his growing responsibilities to his own children, James opened his home to others who needed his support. At one point in 1830, there were twenty-two people in the Forten household.

By the mid-1820s James Forten had become one of the leading men of color in the United States. He spent much of his fortune purchasing slaves their freedom, supporting abolitionist newspapers, offering his home to the Underground Railroad, and opening a school for black children.

From youth to old age, James Forten lived his life with integrity. Following his death on Friday, March 4, 1843, the *United States Gazette* described his funeral procession: "[white mourners] followed [Forten] to his grave as a token of their regard for the excellency of his character. He had won the respect of men of all persuasions, and all shades of complexion."[2]

Levi Coffin (1798–1877)

President of the Underground Railroad

Levi watched as the slave dealer positioned himself in the best spot to keep an eye on his slaves. Levi felt his face flush with anger at seeing these men in shackles. He wanted to talk to them and find out where they were from and where they were going. When the dealer finally went inside for supper, fifteen-year-old Levi took his chance.

Skirting the pile of corn, he stepped near and spoke to several of the slaves. He quickly learned that one named Stephen had been a free man in the North, but while he was sleeping at an inn one night, slave traders had gagged, bound, and placed him in a closed carriage and hurried him into Virginia, where he had been sold to a slave dealer. Now he was on his way south.

Levi was furious. He knew that he could help Stephen if only he could find someone to vouch for his story. Levi ran and hid before the slave dealer returned and ordered Stephen and the others to move on. Would Levi get a chance to help free Stephen? If he was caught helping a slave, it could mean a gigantic fine or, worse, imprisonment. But standing by and doing nothing was not an option for Levi.

Levi Coffin inherited his hatred for slavery from his Quaker father, who was also named Levi. The Quakers believed that every person was equal in God's sight. No man, regardless of race, should be treated with disrespect. The Quakers also believed that knowingly buying stolen goods was the same as stealing them yourself. Since slaves were stolen from their homes and forced to come to America, anyone who bought a slave was a thief.

Born in 1798, Levi lived on a farm in New Garden, North Carolina, with his parents and six sisters. Unable to let his son go to public school because he was needed on the farm, Levi's father educated him at home.

At the beginning of the nineteenth century, the United States was in the midst of a great political debate over the issue of slavery. Northern states passed laws against slavery and abolitionists urged the United States federal government to outlaw slavery in Southern states as well. Most slavery critics supported a gradual end to the institution, hoping to avoid any social turmoil that might occur.

In the Southern states, the economy depended on slave labor. The South was less industrial than the North, and Southern wealth was invested in agriculture, cotton, tobacco, and corn. African-Americans made up about 40 percent of the population and of those, over 90 percent were slaves. Many citizens, including plantation owners, resented interference from the North and passionately defended their right to own slaves. In 1806 Congressman Peter Early of Georgia said, "A large majority of the people in the Southern states do not consider slavery a crime. They do not consider it immoral to hold human flesh in bondage."[1] But Levi Coffin's family could not have disagreed more.

Levi was seven when, while helping his father cut wood near their North Carolina farm, he watched a group of chained slaves slowly shuffle down the road. Levi's father asked them why they had to be chained together. "They have taken us away from our wives and children, and they chain us lest we should make our escape and go back to them,"[2] one said. The reply shocked young Levi.

As the slaves hobbled away, Levi asked his father why the men had been taken away from their families. His father described the realities of slavery, and young Levi's heart grieved for the families torn apart.

Throughout his childhood, Levi continued to witness how slavery demoralized and humiliated its victims. Levi's hatred of slavery grew, and he was determined to do something to help its victims.

His first opportunity to help free a slave came when he was fifteen, at a corn-husking party on his neighbor's farm. One of the guests, a slave dealer named Holland, arrived with a group of slaves. He was on his way south to sell them in the slave markets.

When the supper bell rang, everyone except the slaves and Levi went inside to eat. After listening to Stephen's story of being kidnapped in Baltimore and forced to travel to the slave markets in the South, Levi decided to try and help. With the aid of his father, he collected what information he could about Stephen's friends in the North, promising to try and locate them so that they could testify that Stephen was a free man.

Levi found Stephen's friend Hugh Lloyd who, with other volunteers, followed Stephen's trail to Georgia, where they eventually found him and helped him obtain his freedom. Thanks to Levi, Stephen was freed and allowed to return home.

Throughout his teenage years, Levi often helped runaway slaves who hid in the woods surrounding his hometown. Mounted officers regularly patrolled the roads, knowing that the area was a hideout for runaway slaves. Levi knew that helping runaways was a crime under Southern law. In North Carolina, the penalty was up to a one thousand-dollar fine and six months in prison.[3]

Undeterred, Levi often wandered down the road carrying a sack of corn over one shoulder, pretending that it was feed for hogs that his father and the other farmers in the area allowed to roam in the woods. If the road was clear, he called to the hidden slaves. While the hungry men, women, and children ate the bacon and corn bread hidden in his bag, he listened to their stories of harsh masters and cruel treatment. Whenever possible, he showed them the safest route north.

One fall, when Levi was twenty-one, a former slave named Jack moved near New Garden. Jack's master had died and in his will had granted Jack his freedom; however, distant relatives seized the property and filed a lawsuit to contest the will. The court sided with the relatives and ordered Jack to return to slavery. A one hundred-dollar reward was issued for his capture. Frightened, Jack went into hiding at Levi's house, and Levi convinced his uncle to take Jack to Indiana, where he could safely travel farther north.

Levi eventually left North Carolina but continued his work helping slaves escape the South. He married Catharine White in 1824, and they moved to Newport, Indiana. Levi's house in Newport became a central "station" on the Underground Railroad, a secret network of people working as "conductors" who showed slaves the way to freedom in the North. Houses like Levi and Catharine's provided runaway slaves with a safe place to rest and get help on their journey.

As the country inched towards civil war, the number of fleeing slaves increased. Levi's home became even busier, helping more than one hundred slaves each year. Levi was an upstanding member of the community and his thriving business and reputation deflected opposition to his suspected activities. He even managed to get many of his neighbors involved in helping with the Underground Railroad.

Slave hunters became suspicious and frequently searched the house but found nothing. Luckily Levi and Catharine had created many hidden compartments in the house where people could hide during these searches. The Coffins were so clever at hiding people that every slave who entered their Newport home eventually reached freedom.

In 1847 Levi moved to Cincinnati, Ohio, and opened a warehouse that supplied goods to free-labor businesses. He continued to help on the Underground Railroad, assisting another 1,300 slaves to escape. More than one hundred thousand fugitives escaped via the Underground Railroad in the years between the Revolutionary War and the Civil War; more than three thousand of them had had Levi's help. Eventually Levi's name became so well known among fleeing slaves and slave hunters that he was referred to as the president of the Underground Railroad.

After the Civil War, Levi worked diligently for the Western Freedmen's Aid Society, an organization that helped educate and support former slaves. Levi traveled around the world for the Society, giving speeches and raising more than one hundred thousand dollars. In August 1867 Levi became the U.S. delegate to the International Anti-Slavery Conference in Paris.

On May 14, 1874, Ohio celebrated the adoption of the 15th Amendment to the Constitution of the United States. The amendment granted black citizens the right to vote. At the close of the celebration, Levi Coffin was introduced to the gathered crowd. In his speech he said, "I held the position of president of the Underground Railroad for more than thirty years. I accepted the office thus conferred upon me, and ha[ve] endeavored to perform my duty faithfully. Government ha[s] now taken the work of providing for the slaves out of our hands. The stock of the Underground Railroad ha[s] gone down in the market, the business [is] spoiled, the road [is] of no further use. I resign my office and declare the operations of the Underground Railroad at an end."[4]

Levi died on September 16, 1877, in Cincinnati. His house in Newport stills stands as a museum about the Underground Railroad and a monument to Levi's incredible work.

"I felt no condemnation for anything that I had ever done for the fugitive slave . . . I had no fear of the danger that seemed to threaten my life and business. If I was faithful to duty, and honest and industrious, I felt that I would be preserved."[5] —Levi Coffin

Louis Braille (1809–52)

Inventor for the Blind

Louis gripped his father's hand and stepped hesitantly out of the carriage. The sounds and smells around him were unfamiliar and harsh. The calls of men selling goods in the streets, the cries of beggars pleading for food, and the aroma of baking bread mixed with the rancid, bitter smell of garbage were all frightening. This was Paris, a world away from the fresh air and gentle sounds of his country village.

Louis felt his father's hand tremble as the massive doors opened before them and the director asked them to enter. For months, Louis's parents had argued that he should continue his education at home, but they finally yielded to pressure from Dr. Guillié of the Ministry of the Interior and now Louis was here—at the Royal Institute for Blind Juveniles.

The Director dipped his quill into the inkwell and Louis heard the scratches as the man registered, "Louis Braille, age ten, admitted this day of our Lord, 15 February, 1819."

With an "au revoir" and a quick hug, his father walked away, promising to return for him in August. Once in the dormitory, Louis set his bags on the floor and sat on the bed. He couldn't help but wonder what would happen next.

Louis Braille was born in the fourth hour of the fourth day of January 1809 in the village of Coupvray, twenty-five miles east of Paris. As a toddler, Louis loved watching his father pound leather into beautiful saddles and harnesses and playing at his father's workbench, surrounded by the smells of oil, wood, and new leather.

One day when his father was out of the room, three-year-old Louis picked up a tool and set in motion a series of events that would change his life forever. Somehow his tiny fingers lost their grip on a sharp instrument and it cut into his right eye, severely damaging it. In the weeks that followed, the injured eye infected the other and Louis went completely blind.

Louis quickly adapted to his loss of sight. He created a mental map of his family's cottage in his mind and was soon moving about with ease. From there he ventured into the streets and learned to depend on sound, smell, and touch for guidance.

Education began early for Louis. His father pounded upholstery studs into wooden blocks to form the letters of the alphabet. With the tips of his fingers, Louis traced the metal studs to learn the shape of each letter. Day after day he recited what was on the blocks. Soon he was arranging the letters to form simple words and writing in wavering script with pencils and pens.

When his father had taught him all that he could, it was time for Louis to attend school. At first his brother or sister led him to the one-room school, but soon he was negotiating the cobblestone streets on his own. Louis had a superb memory and registered every fact. He excelled at all his oral examinations and was held back only by his inability to read textbooks and write on his own.

The desire to further their son's education finally convinced Louis's parents to send him to the Royal Institute for Blind Juveniles. On a February morning in 1819, ten-year-old Louis climbed into the coach that would take him to Paris and to the school where he would spend the rest of his life.

For five years, Louis lived and studied in the mildew-covered school. Conditions there were deplorable. Students slept on straw mattresses in a cold, damp dormitory. Awakened each day at six, Louis was given only bread and water for breakfast. He attended morning prayers and was in class by seven. There was a break for a midday meal, which was usually a small bowl of soup, a bit of meat, and, twice a week, a small glass of wine.

Every other Sunday, the soup was replaced by mutton, roast, or veal and the students were given a larger portion of vegetables. Classes continued in the afternoon and ended by eight in the evening. If Louis misbehaved, the punishment was either a beating or solitary confinement, often for days at a time.

Hour after hour, day after day, Louis's fingers traced the raised letters on each page of the huge books designed for blind students. His fingers moved quickly along the legs of an *A*, pausing only briefly to decide if the next letter was a *C* or a *G*. Raised letters took up a lot of room on the page and a single book could be divided into as many as twenty sections, each weighing as much as twenty pounds. The book design and letter-by-letter reading slowed the pace of learning. Louis found the books frustrating because they were so awkward to read.

His teachers and fellow students recognized that he was a genius and that he hungered for more knowledge than he could gain through the school. At twelve years of age, Louis wanted to do something to help overcome the difficulties of his blindness, but his resources were few.

Change eventually came when the school hired a new director who was horrified at the appalling living conditions of the students. To the students' relief, the new director made drastic changes in lifestyle and curriculum. As he searched for improvement in his students' learning, the director chose Louis to review a new form of "night reading" designed by a military captain for passing orders to troops on the battlefield at night. The method used raised dots and bars in vertical lines that stood for words.

Louis and several other students greeted the new idea with enthusiasm, but its shortcomings soon became apparent. Louis pointed out that the new method was only a shorthand for identifying words. What the blind students really needed was a method that would work like the visual written alphabet, a system built on phonics, a system in which the reader was not dependent on memorization but could independently sound out words.

Louis knew that there had to be a way for the blind to read as quickly as the sighted. He wanted all blind people to have access to the same information as sighted people and the ability to read all forms of literature, to record thoughts on paper, and to create stories, poems, and even music.

For months fifteen-year-old Louis pondered this problem. His determination drove him to work long into the night, often catching only moments of sleep. The breakthrough came when he realized that the eyes may see letters on the printed page but it is the brain that interprets them and turns them into understandable information. What he needed was a touch alphabet so that, instead of the eyes, the fingers would "see" the letters and the brain would then interpret them just as it does for sighted people.

In the summer of 1824, Louis invented the Braille cell. The cell consisted of six dots, set in different sequences. Each cell represented a different letter of the alphabet, a numeral, or a punctuation mark. Using the idea of raised dots, he worked backwards, from right to left, punching holes into paper, searching for a simple way to make the dots small enough for the fingertips to gently race across the page.

Louis unveiled his new alphabet at the Institute that fall. The students embraced the beautiful simplicity of the Braille code and quickly memorized the sixty-three configurations of dots and dashes. Before long Louis and his friend Gabriel Gauthier realized that for the code to be successful, they had to find a way for the students to precisely punch the code into paper. Together, they designed a board, about the size of a normal school slate, that allowed a blind student to write. By placing a piece of paper under a sliding grid and working from right to left, the student could feel a letter and then punch it into the paper. When finished, the student would pull out the paper and turn it over, and anyone could read his work. This invention opened up a world of creative expression. Finally the students could take notes in class or write essays, stories, and poetry.

Louis continued to refine his code, searching for ways to make it easier and faster to use. In 1826, at age seventeen, his eight years at the Institute as a student ended and his life as a teacher began. He taught geography, grammar, history, and arithmetic, supervised the slipper-making workshop, and gave piano lessons. Louis's easy-going personality and quiet reasoning manner made him a favorite among his students. One student, Hippolyte Coltat, said, "He conducted his lessons with deep understanding of the special problems of the blind and he taught with such charm . . . The students hung on his words . . . His classes became such a pleasure . . . [The students] saw him as a wise and trusted friend."[1]

At age twenty, Louis unlocked the code for music and mathematics. For the first time, a blind student could read and compose musical scores and write mathematical equations. In 1837, after two years of intense effort by Institute students and teachers, the first full-length book in Braille was published.

In 1841 former student Francois-Pierre Foucault returned to the Institute. He studied Louis's code and wondered how he could help students write Braille more quickly than using the punch method. An inventor, he took one of Louis's ideas and his own mechanical skills and set out to design a machine that was like a typewriter. In late summer 1847, after years of trial and error, he walked into the Institute and proudly handed his machine to Louis. Delighted, Louis ran his fingers over the keys, gently touching each one. He knew that Foucault's keyboard printer was a giant step forward in communication for the blind.

Louis contracted the deadly disease of tuberculosis at the age of twenty-six and spent seventeen years fighting the illness. For most of his adult life, he struggled to perfect the Braille code and make it available to blind students around the world. On January 6, 1852, while Paris celebrated the return of a Napoleon to power, forty-three-year-old Louis Braille died. Because of his determination and indomitable spirit, today many of the estimated 180 million blind people worldwide use the Braille code.

"[Braille] allows blind people to record secret thoughts, to put on paper their impressions and feelings . . . If we blind people were not held back by the characteristic modesty of the author of this system, then we would proclaim him the Jean Gutenberg of the blind!"[2] —Hippolyte Coltat, friend of Louis Braille and fellow student at the Institute

Manjiro Nakahama (1827–98)

Japanese Ambassador

Standing at the edge of the land, fourteen-year-old Manjiro closed his eyes, absorbing the sound of the waves as they crashed against the rocks. Visions of his mother flashed through his mind—her smile when he returned home from fishing, her fingers deftly preparing an evening meal. Every bone in his body ached. Longing to be back in Japan, Manjiro feared that he might die on this deserted island.

For five long months, he and the other members of the shipwrecked fishing crew had hoped for rescue. Now, with the change of seasons, the birds and fish were gone and the rains were ending. Without fresh water and food, there was little chance of survival.

As Manjiro stared out over the vast sea, a small black dot appeared on the horizon. He watched intently as a ship took shape and slowly drew closer to the island. Screaming to his friends, he led the race to the top of a cliff. They watched as the ship dropped anchor and several men lowered two small boats into the water.

As the strangers drew closer, Manjiro noticed that several of them had hair as red as fire. He had never seen such strange people! The rescuers beckoned them to come down from the cliff. The others backed away in fear, but Manjiro knew that this was their only chance for rescue. He quickly descended the rocks and approached the men. Bowing to the ground, Manjiro wondered if they would strike him dead.

Manjiro Nakahama was born in 1827, the tenth year of the Japanese Bunsei Era. He lived in the small fishing village of Nakanohama, on the southern coast of Japan where the warm *Kuroshio*, or black current, from the Pacific Ocean crashes against the rocky shore. His father died when he was nine and his older brother was too weak to work. Manjiro helped his mother earn a living for his brother and four younger sisters. For long hours each day, he sat in a boat and unhooked fish from lines to earn money for his family.

One January morning in 1841, fourteen-year-old Manjiro woke at dawn and set out to sea with four other fishermen in search of sea bass. The boat was loaded with rice, firewood, and fresh water so that they could fish for many days. After traveling twenty-eight miles, they cast their nets but didn't catch a single fish. Day after day, they spread the nets or cast out rods and lines, but their luck never changed.

Unwilling to return home empty-handed, the group kept fishing. On the seventh day, the fishermen sailed into a school of mackerel and sea bream so large that it turned the ocean deep purple. After sending six nets into the water, the excited crew began pulling in an enormous catch.

Suddenly storm clouds billowed on the horizon, the sky darkened, and the winds increased. Waves swelled, rain fell, and a dense fog engulfed them. Exhausted and soaked to the skin and their oars torn away, the fishermen surrendered control of the vessel and hung on for their lives.

When the sea calmed down, Manjiro and his companions struggled to survive on the boat. For five days, they fought the bitter cold by burning small pieces of wood and huddling under a straw mat. When the men's drinking water ran out, they scraped sleet off the boat and licked the tiny icicles that formed on their clothing. When their rice ran out, they caught and ate live fish from the sea.

Finally the men spotted a small island surrounded by massive cliffs and sharp rocks. As the tiny boat approached the land it capsized in the billowing waves, throwing all five men into the frigid water. Bruised and beaten, they crawled onto the rocky shore. With despair, they watched their vessel crash apart against the cliffs. They were stranded.

For the next five months, Manjiro and his friends struggled to keep their bodies and spirits alive. Manjiro spent his days searching for water, hunting the albatross that nested on the cliffs, and fishing. Then one day he spotted a ship on the horizon. He rushed to gain its attention, bravely approached the strange-looking foreign men, and helped rescue his emaciated friends from the island.

Their rescuers were sailors from the United States whaling ship *John Howard*. As the tiny island disappeared from their view on the boat, Manjiro wondered if he would ever see his homeland again. Japan was a closed society; its people were forbidden to leave its islands. Even a fisherman lost at sea could face severe punishment and possibly death if he returned after an extended period of time.

Manjiro spent the next months aboard the ship learning to speak English and helping the crew hunt whales and sea turtles. His determined spirit and strong work ethic caught the attention of the ship's captain, William Whitfield, and made Manjiro a favorite with the crew.

When the *John Howard* reached Hawaii, Captain Whitfield asked Manjiro if he would like to continue on to America. Manjiro knew little about the great country that lay so far away from his home, so with great excitement, he said good-bye to his friends and embraced his new adventure. With hope that Japan's isolation policy would one day end, he decided to learn all that he could about people and cultures different from his own. He thought that one day he would return to Japan and teach his people about the world beyond their borders.

Captain Whitfield gave Manjiro the English name of John Mung, and at age sixteen, Manjiro arrived in New Bedford, Massachusetts. He was amazed by what he saw: a bustling town filled with strange brick houses, huge white churches, and beautiful green parks. What a contrast it was to the rocky coastlines, fishing villages, and thatched huts of his home village in Japan.

Manjiro attended school for the first time in his life and quickly learned to read and write English. At the private Stone School, he met a teacher named Jane Allen, who encouraged him to read English by lending him all the books he wanted. Soon he added mathematics and land surveying to his coursework. A few of the students thought him strange at first, having never seen a Japanese person before, but Manjiro's friendly personality quickly won them over.

Unfortunately not everyone welcomed the newcomer. Some people teased him because he was a foreigner. At church, the deacons told Captain Whitfield that Manjiro couldn't attend Sunday School because he wasn't white. Despite the prejudice, Manjiro did everything he could to learn about the country.

When he turned nineteen, he was asked to join the crew of the whaling ship *Franklin*. Seeing it as an opportunity to hone his nautical skills and possibly find a way to return to Japan, he accepted the offer.

After saying good-bye to his adopted family and friends in America, he spent the next several months harpooning whales, encountering cannibals, and even wrestling a ten-foot sea turtle! One day while sailing off the southern coast of Africa, a huge turtle swam near the starboard side of the ship. The crew, thinking that it would make an excellent turtle soup, sent a harpoon into its body. The turtle, fighting for its life, struggled violently and refused to surrender. To the delight and amazement of the crew, Manjiro took off his clothes, jumped into the sea, and swam over to the monstrous turtle. He killed it, tied a rope around its neck, and let the crew haul it on deck. Manjiro's courage earned him the respect and admiration of the entire crew of the *Franklin*.

During his travels, Manjiro tried several times to return to Japan. He was desperate to see his mother, brothers, and sisters and to convince his country that it should no longer remain isolated from the rest of the world. He wanted to introduce Japan to steam engine trains, telegraphs, and photography. By convincing the government to open Japan's ports to foreign trade, Manjiro hoped to increase the people's standard of living and slowly teach his fellow countrymen about the benefits of a democratic society.

Finally in 1849, at the age of twenty-two, he devised a plan to return home. First he joined the wave of men searching for gold in the California mountains. It took forty days of gold prospecting to earn the six hundred dollars he needed to pay for his journey. With money in hand, he secured passage to Honolulu. In Hawaii he convinced the captain of the *Sarah Boyd* to employ him until they reached the Ryukyu Islands, southeast of the Japanese mainland.

Four miles from the islands, Manjiro and two of his friends lowered a small sailboat, *Adventure*, into the sea. As the *Sarah Boyd* sailed towards the western horizon, Manjiro directed his sailboat towards the rocky Japanese shore. Braving a stormy night at sea near the cliffs, they safely reached land at dawn. After walking to the nearest Japanese village, Manjiro told his story and turned himself in to the local officials, who quickly escorted him and his friends to the town of Naha. After intense interrogation, Manjiro was imprisoned for more than seven months for leaving Japan. Then the eminent Lord Shimazu Nariakira questioned him for six weeks about every detail of his life abroad. He was especially interested in Western inventions like steamships, telegraphs, and photography.

After nine long months of imprisonment, Manjiro was finally allowed to visit his family. On the afternoon of October 5, 1852, Manjiro ended his twelve years of exile. The villagers rejoiced at his homecoming, and that evening a feast of fresh fish and rice was prepared in his honor. As a contented Manjiro sipped sake, he knew that he was finally home.

Manjiro enjoyed only a brief three-day reunion with his family. A messenger arrived with a request that he become an instructor of English, science, and culture at one of the clan schools in Tosa. Manjiro saw the appointment as an opportunity to teach his countrymen about the world beyond Japan's borders.

Many of his students were hungry for knowledge of the outside world and later became important politicians and businessmen. Among them were Iwasaki Yataro, founder of the Mitsubishi corporation; Sakamoto Ryoma, a leader of the revolution that changed Japan from feudal territories into a unified democracy; and Goto Shojiro, a famous politician in the Meiji government.

When Admiral Matthew Perry and his fleet of four United States Navy ships sailed into Tokyo Bay on July 8, 1853, carrying a message from President Millard Fillmore, demanding that Japan open its ports to American ships, Japan was thrown into turmoil. Perry refused to deliver the president's message to anyone but the most highly ranked official. Two princes representing the emperor received Perry, accepted the message, and demanded that his ships leave Japanese waters and return later for a response.

A message was sent to Manjiro in Tosa, requesting that he come immediately and help with this crisis of national security. The government officials desperately needed his knowledge of the English language and American culture. When Perry returned in February 1854, Manjiro interpreted the negotiations that led to the signing of a treaty that opened two Japanese ports to trade with the United States.

Over the following years, Manjiro served as an interpreter and advisor for the Japanese government. In 1860 he returned to the United States with a delegation for the signing of a trade agreement between the two countries. On February 5, 1860, Colonel Brook, who was traveling with Manjiro, entered into his diary, "I am delighted that it was our John Manjiro [who] contributed more than any other person to the opening of Japan."[1]

For the rest of his life, Manjiro served as Japan's first ambassador. He assisted in drawing up plans for large sailing vessels, trained sailors for the navy, and devoted much of his time to translating books on navigation, astronomy, and ship maintenance. In return, Manjiro was given an annual income and other privileges. In his later years, Manjiro settled into a quiet life filled with the joys of children, grandchildren, and his books. Manjiro died on November 12, 1898, at the age of seventy-one and was buried in Tokyo.

Although he is a legend in Japan, few people in the United States know of Manjiro and his remarkable journey. He was the first Japanese person to visit the United States and return to Japan without being severely punished for breaking Japanese isolation laws. Manjiro devoted his life to teaching his countrymen about the outside world. His courage and dedication to his country are an inspiration to today's Japanese children.

Manu (Lakshmibai), Rani of Jhansi (1835–58)

Hero of India's First War for Independence

Heat from the summer sun pounded on seven-year-old Manu's head covering. As sweat trickled down her spine, she rubbed her eyes and strained to focus on the street ahead. Dust swirled under the feet of passing horses and a myriad of sounds in the marketplace made her feel dizzy and sick to her stomach. How she longed for a cool drink of water and a bit of shade. She found a small spot under the edge of a canopy and crouched down. Smiling, she counted the toes on sandaled feet that shuffled by. The heat made her sleepy, and her eyelids began to droop.

Suddenly a scream jolted her to her feet. Running into the street, she saw women and children racing towards her and a wild elephant following closely behind them. As everyone around her struggled to get out of the way, Manu stood in the elephant's path.

Her mouth went dry as she felt the vibration of the huge animal's heavy footsteps. Its trunk swung back and forth and its long ivory tusks gleamed in the sunlight. Although it stayed in the center of the road, Manu knew that if it was suddenly surprised, it would charge into the crowds gathering along the street.

Closer and closer the elephant came. Manu stood perfectly still, waiting for the perfect opportunity. Just as the elephant stepped near, it dropped its head and slowed its pace. Manu grabbed onto a tusk and the elephant lifted her off the ground. Manu stared into its eyes and began to speak in gentle tones.

To everyone's amazement, the animal stopped to listen. For several minutes, Manu hung there, whispering into the giant elephant's ear.

Manu was born on November 21, 1835, in the holy city of Varanasi, into a wealthy, high-caste Indian family. Most couples in India would have wanted a boy, but her father, Moropant Tambe, and her mother, Bhagirathi Bai, adored their new baby girl. They named her Manukarnika, a name for the holy River Ganges, but everyone called her Manu.

On the day Manu was born, her father had her astrological signs read and was amazed when he heard her horoscope: "The newborn girl to whom this horoscope belongs is going to become a queen. She will bestow immortal fame on her husband's clan."[1]

In the nineteenth century it was customary for high-caste Indian families to give daughters away in marriage, even if they were as young as eight years old. These marriages were designed to secure the daughter's future support and status in society. The couple did not actually live together as husband and wife until after the girl reached adulthood (around fourteen years old). So as Manu approached her eighth birthday, the search for a husband began. At about that same time, a courtier from the kingdom of Jhansi named Tatia Dikshit traveled to Bithur in search of a bride for his king, Gangadhar Rao.

Jhansi was a tiny independent kingdom in northern India. It was only one hundred miles wide and sixty miles long, but it was a major center for Indian trade. In the Treaty of Poona, signed by Baji Rao, the king of Delhi, in 1817, the British East India Company agreed not to interfere with the Jhansi monarchy and let it rule the kingdom as it saw fit.

Manu's father was eager to introduce Tatia to his daughter. Manu pleased the courtier and he offered a proposal of marriage on behalf of the king. Her father happily accepted and the courtier returned to Jhansi with the wonderful news that a new queen had been found. It would be the king's second marriage, his first wife having died, and he was delighted to hear of Manu's spirited and fearless nature.

When the wedding preparations were complete, Manu watched in amazement as rows and rows of mounted riders came galloping into Bithur. They escorted her to Jhansi, and as she entered the city, the citizens greeted her with enthusiasm.

On her wedding day in May 1842, the city gates were adorned with garlands of leaves and flowers and the streets glittered with lights. The king's favorite elephant, dressed in gold brocade, roamed the city, waving his trunk. Arabian horses galloped through town, and there was a one hundred-gun salute. The whole country celebrated this special day.

According to Indian custom, Manu changed her name to Lakshmibai, a name given to her by her husband's family at their marriage, and became *rani* (queen) of Jhansi. Lakshmibai embraced her new role as queen. She learned the customs and rules of her new family and, with the help of her ladies, enjoyed learning to make pickles, chutney, and decoratively sliced fruits. She studied Jhansi worship ceremonies and was put in charge of the royal library. Lakshmibai was an excellent equestrian who often practiced with weapons. She even trained a regiment of women and encouraged them to join the army.

Lakshmibai's husband was a good ruler and the people thought that their queen was generous and kind. In 1851, at the age of sixteen, she gave birth to the couple's only child, a boy named Damodar Gangadhar Rao. Unfortunately the boy died only three months later. The king and queen were devastated. After the death of his child, the king began to suffer from fevers and stomach problems.

With his health deteriorating, he expressed a desire to adopt a son to rule Jhansi after him. Two years later, on November 20, 1853, the couple adopted five-year-old Ananda, son of Vasudev, a member of the king's extended family. The next day, on the queen's eighteenth birthday, the king died and all of Jhansi grieved.

Immediately upon the king's death, the British government seized control of the kingdom. Alone and unprepared for this tragedy, Lakshmibai gathered her courage and remembered her responsibility to the people of Jhansi. Lakshmibai was about to face the crisis of her life. Should she give up control of the kingdom to the British or fight for the right of her adopted son to rule?

Lakshmibai chose to fight. First she sent several letters to the British government requesting that they recognize her son as the rightful heir and ruler of Jhansi. On the morning of March 16, 1854, a messenger arrived with the British response.

The scent of burning incense blended with the fragrance of flowers as Lakshmibai sat behind a screen at the end of the grand hall, holding her son in her lap. According to custom, the screen was there to protect her from being viewed by the male representative of the British government. She listened intently as he told her that the British would not recognize her son as the legitimate ruler to the Jhansi throne and declared that Jhansi would now become a part of the British colony in India. They offered Lakshmibai a monthly pension and the right to live in the palace. Lakshmibai was shocked by this blatant attempt to grab her son's kingdom. But how could she fight the British Empire when Baji Rao and other rulers in India were bowing before it?

When the British seized control of Jhansi, they showed the citizens of Jhansi little respect. First they forced the royal army to disband and throw their weapons into the palace well or the Betwa River. Then when the queen planned a pilgrimage to honor her dead husband, they refused her permission to leave Jhansi, making her a prisoner in her own country.

Lakshmibai and her people stood in silent grief as the flag of Jhansi descended from the south tower of the royal fort and the British flag rose in its place. Further humiliation came when the beloved queen was forced to repay the kingdom's past debts. Debt repayment and the need to support her dependants practically bankrupted Lakshmibai. And in order to satisfy the dietary needs of eighty Englishmen, the British opened a beef slaughterhouse in the heart of Jhansi, mortifying the Hindu citizens, who believe that cows are sacred animals.

As a final insult, the British refused to give Lakshmibai the money needed to perform the sacred Hindu Thread Ceremony for her son. An important ritual, the Thread Ceremony is performed around the age of seven and signals the beginning of the "studying" phase of a young boy's life. In the ceremony, three strands of thread are knotted together, symbolizing three entities: the soul, the body, and the Supreme Lord. This insult burned deep in Lakshmibai's heart.

At the same time, all of India suffered under British rule. From the

Indian, and especially Lakshmibai and her people's, point of view, British occupation had become unbearable. In May 1857 rebellion broke out. It quickly gained momentum, moved from northern to central India, and soon reached Jhansi.

Within her country, Lakshmibai felt the discontent and worried about the safety of her people. In June 1857 Jhansi *sepoys*—Indians employed as soldiers by the British government—rebelled. Angry sepoys burned and looted anything that was a symbol of British authority. English men, women, and children fled to the Jhansi fort and surrendered. Unfortunately the sepoys ignored their surrender and massacred all the British citizens. People from the surrounding countryside joined in the uprising, and control of Jhansi returned to Lakshmibai. On June 12 the sepoys set off for Delhi.

Lakshmibai knew that it would be difficult to restore peace. She also knew that the British would avenge the deaths of their citizens. She strengthened the walls around her fort and assembled an army. Brave men, volunteers from the local population, were determined to fight for freedom, independence, and their queen.

The British attacked Jhansi on March 25, 1858. The tiny kingdom stood face-to-face with the well-equipped British army and its powerful cannons. Lakshmibai and her army fought bravely for two weeks. Then, with help from traitors, the British stampeded the fort in overwhelming numbers. Lakshmibai escaped and fled to the town of Kalpi. The British followed her there, and on May 24, it also fell. The rebels then fled to Gwalior, where they took over the fort and were joined by rebel forces from other parts of India.

The Battle of Gwalior was fierce and bloody. Lakshmibai fought bravely to defend her country. On June 18, 1858, the second day of battle, Lakshmibai suffered a sword blow to the chest and was quickly carried to the rear, where she died. Two days later, according to Hindu custom, her body was burned on a funeral pyre.

In India today, Lakshmibai, Rani of Jhansi is a national hero. On August 15, 1947, ninety years after the rebellion began, India became an independent nation within the British Commonwealth of Nations. India set up its own government and on January 26, 1950, its new constitution went into effect. The great warrior who bravely fought in the first struggle for India's independence will forever be remembered as a symbol of freedom.

"That Queen, so very great was she,
Said she would never let go of Jhansi.
She fought for the sake of her soldiers,
And took the bullets herself.
As long as water in India flows
The Queen of Jhansi will live."[2]
—Popular Indian ballad written by Subhadra Kumari Chauhan

Susie (Baker) King Taylor (1848–1912)

Civil War Teacher and Nurse

Clutching a paper package tightly to her chest, eight-year-old Susie gradually picked up her pace. She grabbed her little brother's hand and held it tight. As she dragged him along, a police officer started following them from the opposite side of the street.

Out of the corner of her eye, Susie saw him stop and stare at them. For one endless minute, he stared. She knew that he was wondering why two black kids were out on the streets so early in the morning. Her heart raced as her brother's fingers slipped out of her sweaty hand.

Then, seemingly satisfied, the officer turned and walked back up the street. With a sigh of relief, Susie told her brother to go on ahead. She watched as he moved down the street, looked around to see if anyone was watching, then slipped through Mrs. Woodhouse's gate.

As he disappeared into the house, Susie noticed two white women strolling down the street. They glanced after her brother and then in her direction. Susie turned and walked away. She couldn't risk drawing any more attention. If anyone became suspicious, all the students at the school and their teachers could be caught and sent to jail.

Staring at the white paper that covered her schoolbooks, Susie fumed with anger. It wasn't fair. It wasn't right. Black children should be allowed to go to school!

Susie Baker was born into slavery on August 6, 1848, at the Grest Farm, located on a small island about thirty-five miles off the coast of Georgia. Her mother worked as a house slave and her father worked in the fields. Susie was a Grest family favorite from the time she was born. When she turned seven, Mr. Valentine Grest set in motion a string of events that would change the course of Susie's life when he allowed her and her younger siblings to leave the farm and live with their Grandma Dolly in Savannah.

In the pre–Civil War South, there were many rules regarding African-Americans. Whether slave or free, they had few rights: They weren't allowed to vote or to travel without permission, and they certainly were not allowed to go to school. Everyone knew that teaching black children to read and write, whether they were slave or free, was against the law in Georgia, but Susie was determined to learn.

Each morning Susie and her little brother hid their schoolbooks in wrapping paper and walked one-half mile to Bay Lane. They separated at the corner and, one at a time, sneaked through the garden gate and into a secret school held in Mrs. Woodhouse's kitchen. Mrs. Woodhouse defied the law and taught more than twenty-five local black children. Susie, the other children, and the teachers risked being fined and possibly imprisoned. Susie loved going to school and she took great care in protecting their secret.

Susie attended Mrs. Woodhouse's school for two years. Then Mrs. Beasley became her teacher and taught her for the next three years. When twelve-year-old Susie learned all that Mrs. Beasley could teach her, she turned to her friend Katie O'Conner for help. Katie was white and attended a convent school. With the permission of Katie's mother, the girls secretly met and Katie shared with Susie everything she learned at school.

While Susie stayed busy with her studies, the United States was moving closer to a civil war. There were many reasons for conflict between the Northern and Southern states, especially when it came to taxes, westward expansion, and slavery. States in the industrial North wanted to focus on building factories, importing goods, and expanding the country's system of roads and canals. They also wanted western territories that entered the union to be slave-free states.

Southern states wanted to focus on agriculture, exporting crops to foreign markets, and expanding plantations into the western territories. Expansion and greater profits meant that western territories entering the union needed to be slave states.

By 1858 the conflict dominated life in every corner of the country and consumed Susie. Southern states became so furious that they began talking about leaving the union and forming their own nation. That fall, during an Illinois senate race, a man named Abraham Lincoln said, "A house divided against itself cannot stand. I believe this government cannot endure, permanently half *slave* and half *free*. I do not expect the Union to be dissolved—I do not expect the house to fall—but I do expect it will cease to be divided. It will become all one thing [a nation that allows slavery], or all the other [a nation where all citizens are free]."[1] And from that message, the battle lines were drawn.

In the fall of 1860 Susie read in all the newspapers that Lincoln was running for president of the United States. Many southern state leaders threatened to leave the union if he won. When Lincoln was elected, South Carolina was the first to secede from the union. By the time that Lincoln took office on March 4, 1861, Mississippi, Florida, Alabama, Georgia, Louisiana, and Texas had joined South Carolina and formed a new nation called the Confederate States of America.

Susie searched for any bit of information she could find about the conflict. She read pamphlets, posters, and newspapers. Each piece of news was interesting and exciting. She read about the death threats that forced President Lincoln to arrive in Washington D.C. secretly and in disguise for his own inauguration. She was disappointed to learn that once he was safely there, he said in his inaugural speech that he did not intend to interfere with slavery in the states where it was legal but that he would put the full power and authority of the Federal government behind keeping the union together.

The newspapers had reported the story when the Confederate States of America demanded its independence. And they screamed the news when, on April 12, 1861, the Confederates attacked and then captured Fort Sumter, a Federal fort off the coast of South Carolina. Three days later, on April 15, Lincoln commanded his troops to take back the fort. The South saw that as a declaration of war. Virginia, Arkansas, North Carolina, and Tennessee joined the Confederacy, and the Civil War began.

Every newspaper Susie sneaked away to read was filled with stories about the events leading up to the war, including articles about antislavery activities in the North. She was fascinated with the idea that so many people were willing to fight to free the slaves, and she dreamed of a world without slavery.

On April 1, 1862, the war reached Georgia. Union soldiers began their attack on Fort Pulaski. From miles away, Susie could feel the vibration of the cannons and hear their resounding blasts. Her grandmother, fearing for Susie's safety, sent her and her younger brother and sister back to the Grest Farm to stay with their parents.

When she arrived at the farm, Susie was surprised to find the Grest family gone and their slaves left behind to tend the property. Days later, her uncle decided to take his family and flee into Union protection. Susie passionately believed that slavery was about to end and wanted to help the Union win the war. Leaving her family behind, she joined her uncle and his family and the flow of slaves from plantations across the South, seeking safety and freedom behind Union lines. Near Fort Pulaski, Susie boarded a Union gunboat on its way south to St. Simon's Island.

The Union controlled the southern coast except for the Port of Charleston. On the outlying islands, the Union army set up camps, patrolled the waters, and kept supplies from entering southern ports.

While aboard the gunboat, Susie met Captain Whitmore. They struck up a conversation, and she astounded him with her vast knowledge and ability to read and write. He was so amazed at her skills that he recommended her to his friend, Commodore Goldsborough. Equally impressed, Goldsborough asked Susie if she would be willing to start a school for black children on the island. Susie gladly accepted, knowing that it would be one important way to help the Union cause. With donated books sent from people in the North, she was soon teaching forty young students during the day and many adults at night. Teaching filled most of Susie's days, but somehow she found the time to fall in love and marry a well-educated man named Edward King.

One Sunday two men raced into the camp and sounded the alarm that Confederate troops were on the island. Ninety black men formed a search party, and following several skirmishes, they successfully forced the Confederates back to the mainland. News of their victory reached President Lincoln, and many scholars believe that it encouraged him to order the formation of black fighting regiments in the Union Army. Many of the men Susie taught became members of the first slave regiment to fight for the Union Army, the First South Carolina Infantry Volunteers, later known as the 33rd Regiment of the United States Colored Troops.

As the war progressed, fifteen-year-old Susie soon found a new and more urgent occupation than teaching. When smallpox broke out on the island, she bravely began attending to the sick, even though the doctors wanted her to stay away because the disease was so infectious. Her compassion and kindness led her to give medical care to seriously injured soldiers and to comfort the dying. She later wrote in her memoir, "Strange how our aversion to seeing suffering is overcome in war . . . How we hurry to assist in alleviating their pain, bind up their wounds, and press the cool water to their parched lips, with feelings only of sympathy and pity."[2]

Then came the day Susie had been waiting for. Dr. W. H. Brisbane, a former plantation owner who had become an abolitionist, stood before the crowd and read the wonderful words of the Emancipation Proclamation. "On the first day of January, in the year of our Lord one thousand eight hundred and sixty-three, . . . I, Abraham Lincoln, president of the United States, . . . do order and declare that all persons held as slaves . . . henceforward shall be free."[3]

For the first time in her life, Susie was free to decide what she wanted to do with her life. She and her husband could travel without permission, read books and write letters without fear of the consequences, and freely work for a brighter future for their children.

Susie followed the 33rd Regiment from assignment to assignment, serving as laundress, teacher, and nurse. When the country's first black hospital opened in Beaufort, South Carolina, the wounded men from the 33rd were sent there. Susie often visited "her boys," comforting them in their pain and loneliness. She said, "All the boys . . . are the same to me as those in my Company E; [they] are all doing the same duty, and I will do just the same for [them]."[4]

Susie spent the rest of the war nursing the wounded and dying. The Civil War finally ended in April 1865. At the age of seventeen, after four years and three months of work and no pay, Susie finally said good-bye to her soldiers and returned to Savannah with her husband.

Susie expected her life to improve, but prejudice against black people was still so widespread that even her husband, a master carpenter, couldn't find work. A year later, he died in an accident, leaving Susie to raise their yet unborn child alone. Despite her troubles, she tried several times to open a private school for black children. Free schools opened in town, however, and she lost her students. In 1874 she moved to Boston and married Russell Taylor in 1879.

Susie dedicated her later years to working for black veterans. She founded Corps 67, the Boston branch of the Women's Relief Corps, a national organization for female Civil War veterans. She served as treasurer and then as president, continually fighting for equal treatment for black veterans. "All this time my interest in the boys in blue has not abated. I was still loyal and true, whether they were black or white. My hands have never left undone anything they could do toward their aid and comfort in the twilight of their lives."[5]

For the rest of her life, Susie struggled in whatever way she could to help the cause of freedom and equality for all people. In 1902 she published her memoirs, hoping to preserve for future generations the true story of the many brave soldiers, both black and white, who sacrificed their lives to end slavery. She never lost hope that one day all people in America would be treated equally. She said, "I know I shall not live to see the day, but it will come—the South will be like the North, and when it comes it will be prized."[6]

"We are similar to the children of Israel, who, after many weary years in bondage, were led into that land of promise, there to thrive and be forever free from persecution . . . What a wonderful revolution!"[7]

—Susie (Baker) King Taylor

Ebba Lund (1924–99)

Savior of Danish Jews During World War II

Walking towards the wharf, nineteen-year-old Ebba quickly picked up her pace and passed through the harbor gate. She took off her red hat and shoved it into her shoulder bag. Only minutes before, she had helped several Jewish families board a fishing boat that would take them to Sweden. She smiled, remembering the look of hope on their faces. After two weeks of helping Jews escape the Nazis, she still felt relief each time a boat safely left the dock.

Spotting two German soldiers patrolling the wharf, Ebba glanced around, hoping for an easy escape. They were walking directly towards her. Fearing that they might demand to inspect her bag, Ebba tucked it tightly under her arm. She had a large amount of money inside and knew that they would arrest her if they found it.

Cold seawater slapped against the weather-grayed pier and Ebba wondered, would the soldiers leave or would they arrest her?

When sixteen-year-old Ebba Lund got out of bed on the morning of April 9, 1940, she had no idea that her world was about to change. Gone would be the quiet days of going to school, spending time with friends at the Tivoli Gardens amusement park, eating at restaurants, taking long bike rides in the country, and going to concerts. After breakfast, she got on her bike and rode along the Copenhagen streets towards school. She was surprised when she ran into a crowd of people surrounding a group of German soldiers.

Moving her bike nearer to the edge of the crowd, she stopped to watch. A man next to her whispered something she had never expected to hear: The Germans had invaded Denmark! Ebba jumped back onto her bike and rode past the British embassy, where another crowd was gathering.

As she watched, German soldiers entered the embassy and forced all the British diplomats into waiting trucks. A German soldier threatened to shoot anyone who tried to escape. His words stunned the crowd into silence. Then in protest against the German soldiers and their occupation and to show her support for the British, Ebba joined the rest of the crowd, chanting, "Hurrah for the Britons! Hurrah for the Britons!"[1]

Germany had invaded Poland seven months earlier on September 1, 1939, and was at war with Great Britain and France. Many in Denmark thought that their nonaggression treaty with Germany would keep them safe from an invasion, but on March 1, 1940, Hitler had revealed his plans for Denmark: "We will do our utmost to make the operation appear as a peaceful occupation . . . If, in spite of this, resistance should be met, all military means will be used to crush it."[2] On April 9, 1940, Germany invaded Denmark.

As Ebba rode back to school, she picked up one of the thousands of green leaflets dropped from German aircrafts over Copenhagen. Addressed to the Danish soldiers and the Danish people, they read, "Attention! Germany is occupying Denmark for your protection, to save you from the evil British and French."[3] But the Danish people knew that they shouldn't fear the British or French. The true enemies were Adolf Hitler and the German army.

Hitler's early morning invasion took Denmark by surprise. Denmark's history of neutrality and its small military, along with no immediate help from Britain and France, led the Danish government to decide to negotiate rather than fight. After only two hours of negotiations, the Danish government agreed to Germany's terms and began a policy of cooperation.

Denmark was important to Hitler's military plans. Danish railroads could transport war materials from Sweden, and its vast agricultural land could supply food for Hitler's army. For the next three years, life did not change much for Ebba and the Danes. King Christian X remained on his throne, the government continued to function, even holding free elections, and Germany seldom interfered; however, German soldiers walked their city streets every day, reminding the Danes who was in control. Few in the country sympathized with the Nazis, and everyone knew that Denmark had lost two important things: its national identity and democratic freedom.

Slowly the Danes began to resent losing control of their own destiny. Many were ashamed of their country's easy surrender, and an active resistance movement was born. A majority of the early resistance was passive. Participants would ridicule German soldiers and gather in public places to sing patriotic songs. Even teenagers began playing pranks, slashing tires on German cars and painting the letter "V" for victory on Copenhagen fences and building walls. One day at a main intersection in Copenhagen, as a German soldier stood in a waist-high circle of sandbags directing traffic, a crowd surrounded him, stopping traffic and laughing at a sign that someone had posted above his head: "Attention! This soldier is not wearing trousers!"[4]

A growing number of people in the resistance, including Ebba, felt that they needed to be more active. Ebba began by distributing a newspaper her sister, Ulla, had secretly printed on an old copying machine. While the rapidly growing illegal press stirred anti-German sentiment, Ebba was busy stealing weapons, setting fire to railroad cars, putting sugar into gasoline tanks, and blowing up the factories that made motors for German submarines.

In September 1942 King Christian X received a birthday greeting from Hitler and his terse reply sent Hitler into a rage. In response, he demanded thirty thousand Danish "volunteer" soldiers and a change in government, and he appointed one of his own men, Erik Scavenius, prime minister.

By the fall of 1943, Germany's troops were overextended, fighting on many fronts around the world. Danish resistance escalated, peaking in August when worker strikes broke out across the nation. On August 28, Germany laid out new demands: no public gatherings, no strikes, an 8:30 PM curfew, and censorship of the press. All attacks on German soldiers, acts of sabotage, and possession of firearms or explosives were punishable by death. The Danish government refused the demands and finally abandoned all cooperation. On August 29, martial law was declared and Denmark went into a state of emergency.

Jewish people across the country realized that they were in grave danger. Besides wanting to dominate Europe and the Soviet Union, Hitler sought to annihilate all Jews and opponents to his regime. Across German-occupied Europe, troops arrested and transported Jews to concentration camps, where they were put to death.

Hitler sent secret orders from Berlin that all Danish Jews were to be sent to the Theresienstadt concentration camp in Czechoslovakia. Two ships scheduled to arrive in Denmark at the end of September would transport them there. On the nights of October 1 and 2, soldiers planned to raid homes, arrest every Jew, and pack them onto the ships. Word of the plan leaked out when German naval attaché Georg Duckwitz told Hans Hedtoft, one of the main leaders of the resistance.

News of the deportation spread quickly. Across the country, Danish citizens were outraged and warned every Jewish person they met. Thousands flocked to hiding places in summer homes, warehouses, barns, and churches. Denmark was united behind the common cause to save their Jewish friends and neighbors.

When the German soldiers raided the homes of known Jews, almost every one of them was gone. And, surprisingly, none of their neighbors knew where they were. Of the nearly eight thousand Jewish people in Denmark, only 464 were caught and sent to Theresienstadt.

By this time, Ebba was nineteen-years-old and had joined a small group of Danish resistance fighters led by Jorgen Kieler. They met in Kieler's apartment or in a bookstore right across the street from Nazi headquarters in downtown Copenhagen.

Keeping thousands of Jews hidden in the small, flat land of Denmark was impossible. The easiest and safest place for them to go was across the Kattegat Strait or the Narrow Sound to the neutral country of Sweden. When Danish nuclear physicist Niels Bohr heard about the roundup of Jews, he fled to Sweden. Once there, he asked the Swedish foreign minister and the king to provide a safe haven for Denmark's Jews. Sweden agreed.

Ebba's resistance group knew that it had to help. First it needed money to pay for transportation and bribes. A young man named Klaus and Keiler's sister Elsebet walked from house to house in the wealthy neighborhoods outside Copenhagen where Klaus had grown up, asking for donations.

Each time they knocked on a door, there was a chance that a German sympathizer would open it. Every request could have led to their arrest, but no one turned them in. By the end of the weekend, they had collected enough money to help hundreds of Jews.

Meanwhile, Ebba turned her attention towards finding a way to safely transport the Jews to Sweden. She knew of a local fisherman who lived in Nordhavn, on the north end of the harbor. When she asked if he would help smuggle Jewish families out of Denmark, he agreed and passed the word along. By morning, there were nearly one dozen fishermen ready to help. They soon established two important escape routes out of Copenhagen.

It wasn't long before Danish Jews started arriving in Copenhagen seeking help. If they went to the bookstore and Kaj Munk's book of poems was visible in the window, it was safe to enter. From there, Ebba escorted them to the harbor. At the entrance to the harbor, they passed several fake guards who were actually resistance fighters dressed in German uniforms to fool the German patrols into thinking that the harbor was secure. Once past the guards, the Jews were to wait until they saw Ebba put on a bright red hat. This was the signal that it was safe to approach the boat. When they reached the water, Ebba helped them onto a boat and paid for their passage.

Ebba's red hat earned her the code name Little Red Riding Hood. She preferred to work during the day, feeling that the Germans would never suspect open resistance in broad daylight. One afternoon, after escorting several passengers to a boat, she ran into a German patrol. If they stopped her and found the money in her shoulder bag, it would raise suspicion and she could be arrested and questioned. Unwilling to risk exposing her fellow resistance fighters, she quickly walked up to one of the fishermen working on the wharf, took his arm, and smiled lovingly into his eyes. The man, noticing the patrol, smiled back and played along with her. The patrol walked away.

Ebba and her resistance friends helped between seven hundred and eight hundred Jews escape the Nazis. In less than two weeks about 7,200 Jews from all across Denmark safely crossed the strait to Sweden. The Danish people helped almost 95 percent of Danish Jews elude capture by the Nazis.

Once the Jews were safely out of Denmark, Ebba and her resistance group began to transport spies, agents, weapons, and secret documents out of Denmark. Then they turned their attention towards sabotage. Hitler was furious over the number of incidents and ordered reprisal killings: Five Danes would die for every German soldier or informer killed. The first victim was Kaj Munk, whose books stood defiantly in Ebba's resistance group's bookstore window. Hitler used intimidation, executions, deportation, and arrests to try to stop the sabotage.

But Hitler's plan to terrorize the Danish people backfired. He only managed to fuel their anger. Ebba's resistance group conducted twenty-five acts of sabotage, dealing a significant blow to the Germans before they were forced to disband.

On May 5, 1945, German forces in Denmark surrendered to the Allies. Ebba was among the enormous crowds celebrating on the streets of Copenhagen that day. Her joy over victory was tempered by the knowledge of the great sacrifices that had been made to obtain it. Of her group of resistance fighters, two were shot in action, two—including Klaus—committed suicide to keep its secrets, four survived deportation, and the others survived underground in Denmark or as refugees in Sweden.

After the war, the Jewish citizens of Denmark returned home to a warm welcome. Unlike other Jews throughout Europe, who had had everything they owned taken away, Danish Jews returned to a life preserved and waiting for them. Their neighbors and friends had watched over their homes, tended their gardens, fed their pets, and kept their businesses running.

Ebba Lund was part of an amazing World War II story. After the war, she married, had three children, and earned a degree in chemical engineering. She worked in Sweden for several years before returning to Denmark to teach. Always determined to help others, Ebba became head of the Department of Virology and Immunology at the Royal Copenhagen Agricultural University. She died in the summer of 1999, but Denmark will never forget her bravery and sacrifice.

Pierre Labiche (1927–Unknown)

French Resistance Fighter During World War II

Fear rushed through thirteen-year-old Pierre as the Nazi officer ordered him to the front of the schoolroom. Unsure of what was about to happen, he stood and slowly moved between the desks. Standing before the officer, Pierre watched the man's lips move, but because he was deaf he couldn't hear a word. Suddenly the officer slapped him across the face with a leather glove. Terrified, Pierre turned towards the schoolmaster, pleading for help, but saw that the teacher was powerless to protect him. The officer's glove came up again and slapped Pierre's other cheek, leaving twin welts on his face. From the corner of his eye, he saw his friend Gabrielle jump up and scream at the officer to stop.

Pierre knew that the officer suspected that he was helping the French Resistance. Somehow he had to convince him that he had spent the entire night at home. Using hand motions, Pierre told his story to the teacher, who translated his words for the officer.

Suspicious blue eyes stared into Pierre's face. Not completely satisfied with Pierre's explanation, the Nazi scanned the room filled with frightened faces, raised his hand, and yelled, "Heil Hitler!"

Pierre breathed a sigh of relief. He had almost been caught!

Born deaf in 1927, Pierre Labiche never learned to talk but could communicate with his family and teachers by using hand gestures. His mother died when he was young, and when his father was called to serve in World War II, twelve-year-old Pierre moved in with his only living relative, his father's aunt, Paulette.

France and Great Britain entered the war on September 3, 1939, two days after Germany invaded Poland. When the German army turned its attention towards invading Luxembourg, the Netherlands, and then Belgium, the people of Pierre's tiny village began to worry. Then on May 10, 1940, the unthinkable happened: Germany invaded France. French forces rushed to attack the advancing troops, but by mid-June, the capital city of Paris fell. On June 22, France surrendered.

Pierre's father was killed during the fierce fighting, and the news reached Pierre a few months later.

Germany occupied the northern two-thirds of France, including Pierre's village near the city of Caen on the Normandy coast. The southern part of the country remained under French control; however, the French leader, Henri Philippe Pétain, paid huge amounts of money and sent large numbers of workers to Germany. He also joined in the persecution of Jews.

In contrast to Pétain, General Charles de Gaulle fled to London and launched a movement called Free France that encouraged the French to battle the Germans in any way they could. This resistance movement spread throughout France and continued to cause problems for Germany until the end of the war.

Following Germany's invasion, Pierre and his aunt endured Nazi control over every aspect of their lives: enforced curfews, occupied homes and businesses, and surveillance of their every move. Before long, thirteen-year-old Pierre and his aunt joined the Free France resistance. Whenever possible, the resistance helped to: rescue French soldiers and British pilots, blow up bridges used to transport German soldiers and supplies, and coordinate bombing raids by relaying troop movements to London. Every effort was made to slow down and frustrate the German army.

Pierre and his aunt lived in a small cottage near the sea. Each day he walked the mile from his home into the village to attend school. He found school a welcome distraction from the realities of Nazi occupation.

After school, Pierre always stopped by the village pharmacist's shop to buy his aunt a small bag of peppermint tea. By keeping this habit, he avoided raising any suspicion among the patrolling German soldiers when the pharmacist had secret messages from the resistance to pass along.

On an October day in 1940, the pharmacist quickly scribbled a note on a strip of paper. He showed it to Pierre. It read, "Tonight, 1:30." Pierre gave a sharp nod to signal that he understood that the British were planning to launch an air attack on German positions that night. Pierre watched as the pharmacist burned the paper.

Later that evening, Pierre stood at his bedroom window and stared into the sky. Never had he seen such darkness. Nothing was visible, not even the stars nor the moon. Suddenly he saw the light of antiaircraft gunfire in the distance. Shots blanketed the sky as searchlights tried to penetrate the dense cloud cover, looking for planes to shoot down.

Pierre intently followed the searchlights, scanning for any sign that a plane might have been hit by German gunfire. For one brief moment, he thought he saw a parachute. Seconds passed. The searchlights wove a pattern across the sky, but there was no further sign of a downed pilot. Pierre's inability to hear or speak had heightened his other senses. His eyesight was far better than anyone else's, and he knew he had seen a falling parachute. Despite the risks to his and his aunt's lives if caught outside after curfew, he had to try to save that pilot.

Pierre quickly left the cottage and slipped into the woods. Sneaking through the trees, Pierre found the pilot struggling to bury his parachute in the ground. Suddenly a pencil-thin beam from the pilot's flashlight shone into Pierre's eyes. The pilot had seen movement in the trees and was reaching for his revolver.

Pierre raised his hands and placed a finger to his lips, imploring the pilot to remain silent. Then he knelt down and started digging. They buried the parachute, covering it with leaves and branches. When they were finished, Pierre grabbed the pilot's hand and led him through the woods. As they approached a neighbor's farm, Pierre abruptly dove into a ditch, pulling the pilot down with him.

As the explosion of bombs rumbled across the earth, Pierre and the pilot crawled along a thick hedge. Several minutes later, Pierre stopped and signaled for the pilot to lie down. Suddenly searchlights lit up the road and the surrounding countryside. The light skipped over Pierre and the pilot, but the truck stopped near their hiding spot. Pierre held his breath as two soldiers quickly searched the area before heading towards the village. Relieved, Pierre led the pilot back to his aunt's house.

Lifting several chunks of wood and sweeping away the dirt, Pierre revealed a cellar door in the floor of the garden shed. His aunt motioned for the pilot to descend into the tiny room. It was small but had a cot and blankets. Pierre watched as his aunt explained to the pilot that they would protect him and try to get help. Then they left him in the dark, damp hole.

The next evening the schoolmaster, Monsieur Duplay, came to visit. Also a member of the resistance, he sat at the kitchen table, writing a letter for Pierre's aunt and memorizing the pilot's identity number so he could report to London that the pilot was alive.

Pierre was surprised when his aunt quickly handed him a toy construction set from the cupboard. That was the signal to act normal and play like a typical little boy. Pierre knew that something was wrong. Suddenly a German lieutenant and his sergeant stormed through the front door and scanned the room. The lieutenant walked over to the table, grabbed the letter, and examined the pages. Pierre watched the lieutenant question Aunt Paulette and Monsieur Duplay and order a search of the house.

Pierre and Monsieur Duplay exchanged glances as Aunt Paulette led the lieutenant up the stairs. When he returned, he explained that his sergeant would live in their spare bedroom. A Nazi living in their own house! Everyone, including the hidden pilot, was in even greater danger of being discovered.

On Thursday evenings, the village choir practiced at the local inn. It was the only time that people were allowed out past curfew and the perfect opportunity to get a message out to the resistance. Pierre always helped serve drinks and wash dishes. After that Thursday's practice, the innkeeper told him to put away the music books and accordion. Pierre quickly gathered them up and climbed to the second floor. Once there, he rapped a prearranged code on a trapdoor in the ceiling. A resistance radio operator hiding above lowered a tiny basket through the trapdoor. Pierre placed a coded message that he had kept hidden in his mouth inside the basket. Pierre raced back to the first floor so that the German guards wouldn't become suspicious.

In the time that it took Pierre to reach the lower floor, the plan for the downed pilot's escape was being transmitted to England. As he walked home, a radio detector truck rushed past, searching for illegal radio signals. Pierre smiled, knowing that they were too late; the wireless operator had been long gone.

Four nights later, Pierre went to the cupboard for his toy construction set, but this time for a different reason. Each night since the sergeant had started living at their house, he and Pierre drank cider and built buildings and bridges together. The sergeant enjoyed this nightly routine and never suspected that his young companion might be part of the resistance.

On this night, Pierre had secretly drugged the sergeant's cider with a sleeping powder. After finishing his second drink, the sergeant dropped his head onto the table and slipped into unconsciousness, the victim of the pharmacist's handiwork and Pierre's ingenuity.

Around eleven, Pierre stood watch while Aunt Paulette greeted two men who had emerged from the woods. The men, dressed in black, spoke quietly while Aunt Paulette led them to the pilot's hiding place. Then, without a sound, the two men and the rescued pilot vanished into the darkness. Pierre and his aunt carried the sergeant to his room and laid him on his bed. He would never know what had transpired that night or how he had fallen asleep so quickly.

Three days later, Monsieur Duplay wrote a few lines from a Victor Hugo poem on the blackboard in class: "The future, the future, the future belongs to me." The poem was a secret message to Pierre: the pilot had arrived safely back in England.

Pierre and hundreds of kids like him spent the rest of the war risking their lives to rescue pilots who were shot down over the French countryside or quietly sabotaging German military forces. In 1944 Pierre and his aunt rejoiced when Allied troops landed on the Normandy coast near their home. The war ended in 1945. Thanks to Pierre and all the others like him who fought against Hitler's forces, the world was finally free from Nazi oppression.

Claudette Colvin (1940–)

Fighter for Black Civil Rights

Claudette flinched when the driver shouted at her, demanding that she move to the black section at the back of the bus. Tired and hungry, she was not about to give up her seat. Why should she stand for the rest of the journey home?

The driver stopped the bus and walked down the aisle. He stood over her, insisting that she move or he'd call the police. Anger surged through thirteen-year-old Claudette. She had a right to sit there and she was not going to move.

The white passengers remained silent, watching and waiting to see what would happen. Two police officers boarded the bus and ordered Claudette to move. She refused.

One of the officers kicked her and the other grabbed her wrist, yanking her from the seat. Amid calls of encouragement from the black passengers, Claudette kicked and screamed as the officers hauled her down the aisle and out onto the street. They shoved her into the back of their squad car and quickly pulled away from the curb.

Handcuffed, Claudette remained silent as the officers hurled abuses at her and called her terrible names. What were they going to do with her? Would they beat her? Would they kill her?

In the year that Claudette Colvin was born, the United States watched as Adolf Hitler began his campaign of conquest across Europe. Two years later, the nation's young men were in the midst of World War II. For another four years, soldiers of every ethnic background fought side by side until they finally returned victorious in 1945. Unfortunately the equal treatment that young black men had experienced in wartime did not translate into equal treatment in peacetime. They returned to a nation thankful for their heroism but unwilling to offer them equality in American society.

Living with her grandmother in Montgomery, Alabama, young Claudette felt the growing wave of discontent among young black citizens. Rebellious by nature, her sense of justice battled with the reality of her daily life. Because she was black, Claudette was not allowed to use the same facilities as whites. She had to drink from a separate water fountain, use a separate bathroom, and sit in the black section on the city bus. The facilities designated for black people were often of poor quality or did not work as well as those reserved for white people. Everywhere she looked there were signs posted that read, "Colored Enter Here" or "For Whites Only." Even the justice system, supposedly designed to protect all citizens' rights, favored whites. A black person often faced a guilty sentence, even if evidence proved otherwise.

Claudette was about nine when she really began noticing the inequality around her. When she asked to go to the rodeo at the coliseum, she learned that it was for white kids only. Her father tried to soften the blow by buying her a cowboy hat, but it could not make up for Claudette's disappointment. At the five-and-ten-cent stores like Kress's or H. L. Green, she could buy merchandise but not sit at the counter and enjoy a soda or a hamburger. In some stores, she couldn't even try on clothes.

While in the ninth grade, Claudette's schoolmate, seventeen-year-old Jeremiah Reeves, was accused of raping a white woman. A very popular student at the all-black Booker T. Washington High School, Jeremiah loved music and played drums in a local band. Many in the African-American community thought that he was innocent and that his confession (which was later retracted) had been coerced. The high school took up a collection, and Claudette helped organize movie nights to raise money for Jeremiah's defense. Unfortunately Jeremiah was sentenced to death for a crime that white men at that time were rarely punished for, let alone ordered to serve a life sentence or given the death penalty. The injustice of the verdict enraged Claudette and the black community.

Unlike Jeremiah, Claudette was not a popular student. She was smart and a year ahead of her peers in school. Influenced by her history teacher, a self-described "real, pure-blooded African," Claudette continued to question Southern society. In essays for class, she explored her feelings about segregation and what it meant to be black in America.

On March 2, 1955, fifteen-year-old Claudette waited for the Highland Gardens bus outside of the Dexter Avenue Baptist Church, where civil rights leader Martin Luther King Jr. served as pastor. It was late, and she was anxious to get home to study for Friday's exams. Carrying heavy schoolbooks, a relieved Claudette watched as the bus approached.

She paid her fare—the same amount as a white rider—up front, but had to board in the back so that she wouldn't walk through the white section. The front ten seats were reserved for white people and the back ten seats for black people. The middle seats were for either, but a black person had to move if a white person wanted the seat.

Claudette sat in one of the middle seats. The bus moved on and passengers began to fill the empty seats. Claudette soon realized that people were staring at her. The white riders expected her to get up and stand at the back of the bus, but she refused to budge.

The bus driver, looking in his rearview mirror, ordered Claudette to move. She just sat, not saying a word. Suddenly all the riders noticed the conflict and became silent. The driver stopped the bus, refusing to continue the route until she moved. White passengers, anxious to get home, began to demand that she get up. Black riders, supporting her from the back of the bus, said that she didn't have to.

The bus driver hailed a traffic policeman and he boarded the bus. He stood over Claudette and demanded that she get up. She looked directly at him and said, "No!" She told the officer that she was as good as any white person and she wasn't going to move.

He left the bus and returned with two other officers. They each demanded that she get up. When she again refused, one of the officers kicked her. Then they each grabbed a wrist, sending her books flying to the floor. She fought with all her strength, kicking, flailing her arms, and screaming, "It's my constitutional right to sit here . . . You have no right to do this!"[1]

The officers dragged her off the bus, slapped handcuffs on her wrists, shoved her into a squad car, and hurled insults at her all the way to city hall. From there, they took young Claudette to the city jail, put her in a cell, and locked the door. A few hours later, her father posted bail.

Claudette was charged with violating the state segregation law, disorderly conduct, and assaulting an officer. Defended by the only black lawyers in the city, Fred Gray and Charles Langford, Claudette soon had her day in court. Two weeks later, she stood before juvenile court judge J. Lister Hill, listening in amazement when he found her guilty, sentenced her to probation, and ordered her to pay a fine.

As her sobs filled the courtroom, Claudette knew deep in her heart that the verdict was unjust. And she wasn't alone. Following reports of her guilty verdict, large numbers of black citizens, in a spontaneous protest, refused to ride the city buses.

Claudette's attorneys appealed her conviction to the Montgomery Circuit Court. On May 6, 1955, the judge upheld the assault charges. The judge succeeded in preventing Claudette's lawyers from using her case to test the constitutionality of the segregation laws.

On October 21, police arrested another young girl, eighteen-year-old Mary Louis. She too defied a bus driver's orders to give her seat to a white person. Then on December 5, a woman named Rosa Parks took matters into her own hands. A member of the National Association for the Advancement of Colored People (NAACP), Parks was a youth leader and Claudette's friend. Inspired by Claudette's bravery, she also defied a bus driver and refused to give up her seat. Arrested and thrown into jail, Parks became the NAACP's long-awaited test case that would prove the injustice of segregation laws.

Leaders in the black community decided to show support for the court case with a bus boycott. Alabama State College English professor Jo Ann Robinson quickly wrote a flier and spent all night mimeographing thousands of copies. The flier called for a one-day boycott of all Montgomery buses. On Monday, December 5, 1955, nearly fifty thousand black people walked, hitchhiked, or carpooled everywhere they went. The buses ran their routes but were virtually empty. The success of that one-day boycott led to an extension that lasted almost one year.

On May 11, 1956, sixteen-year-old Claudette testified in court for *Browder v. Gayle*, a case testing the constitutionality of bus segregation. The hearing lasted five hours, and the papers later reported that Claudette was a star witness. A month later, the judge ruled that Montgomery's segregation laws were unconstitutional. The decision was appealed to the United States Supreme Court, but the verdict was upheld. Montgomery buses and other facilities had to be desegregated.

Today Claudette lives in New York City, works as a nurse's aide, and is the mother of two sons.

The Civil Rights Movement in the United States was born with the *Browder v. Gayle* case and the Montgomery Bus Boycott. Claudette's courage led to the first major court victory for black people and gave others the courage to continue the fight. Her spot in the annals of black history is secure.

"Civil rights wasn't about our skin color; it was as simple as what is right and what is wrong, what is fair and what is unfair."[2] —Claudette Colvin

Mary Beth Tinker (1952–)

Champion for Student Rights

A weak winter sun peeked through the trees as thirteen-year-old Mary Beth entered the doors of Harding Junior High. It was now or never, she thought. She had to go in; the bell was about to ring. Taking one step at a time, she headed to her locker. After hanging up her coat, she touched the black armb and that was securely fastened around her upper arm. She was breaking a school rule. Armbands had been banned, but it was her way of silently protesting the Vietnam War.

All morning she waited for someone to notice the band and tell her to take it off. No one did. Then it was time for the first class of the afternoon, Mr. Moberly's math class. He had spent the previous day telling his students how un-American it was to protest the war. If anyone was going to notice her band, it would be him. Several minutes into class, Mr. Moberly handed her a pass and told her to go to the office. This was it, the time of reckoning. Mary Beth stood and walked out of the room.

The vice principal's desk loomed in front of her. As Mary Beth watched, he looked at the pass, turning it over to see if there was anything written on the back. She stood in silence, waiting for him to seal her fate.

When Mary Beth Tinker was born in the early 1950s in Des Moines, Iowa, the United States was at war in Korea, McDonald's opened its first restaurant in Illinois, and there was finally a vaccine for polio. The American economy was booming, the birth rate was skyrocketing, and the average American was living a good life.

Mary Beth's father, a Methodist minister, and her mother championed various civil liberty and moral causes. Both were also strong antiwar activists. From the time that Mary Beth could hold a picket sign, she attended civil rights and peace demonstrations. The first was a fair housing demonstration in Des Moines when she was about ten. She became personally concerned about politics and peace issues in the fourth grade while writing a report about the atomic bomb dropped on Japan. The next year she wrote a paper on capital punishment.

In 1965 Mary Beth was thirteen, in the eighth grade, popular at school, and an excellent student. The United States was embroiled in the Vietnam War. Every day, across the country, newspapers, magazines, and television covered the conflict. Battle footage and color photographs brought the death and destruction into most American homes. The nation was divided over the issue of whether or not to stay in Vietnam. Should the United States help South Vietnam push back the Communist invader, North Vietnam? Or was the war unjustified, an intervention in the affairs of another country that had too high a human and moral cost?

Congress never officially declared war on North Vietnam, but by the end of 1965, President Lyndon B. Johnson had 170,000 U.S. soldiers stationed in South Vietnam, fighting to hold back the Communist invaders. During the first week in November, the number of United States soldiers killed in the war surpassed one thousand.

Whether a declared war or not, 140 anti–Vietnam War protest groups decided to stage a march on Washington D.C. An estimated twenty-five thousand protesters attended. Among the crowd were about fifty people from Iowa, two of whom were Mary Beth's older brother, John, and her mother, Lorena.

On the ride home from the protest, someone suggested wearing black armbands in protest of America's involvement in Vietnam. The following weekend, as snow blanketed the small Iowa town, Mary Beth and about twenty-five other students and adults met to discuss their antiwar protest plans. They decided that on December 16 the students would begin wearing black armbands to school. The black bands had two purposes: to mourn the death of civilians and soldiers in Southeast Asia and to show support for Senator Robert Kennedy's call for a Christmas truce, which would hopefully lead to negotiations and a cease-fire.

Word of the student protest filtered out and reached the ear of Dwight Davis, the superintendent of the Des Moines schools. He called a meeting with the principals of the five senior high schools and the director of secondary education. They decided to take advanced action and ban armbands from the schools.

On the morning of December 16, Mary Beth was fully aware of the ban when she walked to school wearing an armband over the sleeve of her sweater. She entered Harding Junior High School determined to express her views and feeling that the armband was a nondisruptive way of doing it. She wore her armband to her morning classes, and in her science class she passed around a petition for the right to wear armbands in school. In the lunchroom, a group of boys teased her and several students asked questions and discussed the Vietnam issue.

During math class, Mary Beth's teacher, Richard Moberly, handed her a pass and sent her to the office. She met with the vice principal, who asked her to remove the band. She did and returned to class; however, a few minutes later, Mary Beth's advisor asked to see her. Once they were back in her office she told Mary Beth that she was suspended from school and sent her home.

That evening, twenty-five students and their parents met to discuss a response to the suspension of Mary Beth and a high school student named Christopher Eckhardt. They were the only students who had worn their bands even after the principals had banned them.

The group decided to protest at the next school board meeting on December 21. By the end of the week, three more students, including Mary Beth's brother, had been suspended for wearing armbands.

News of the protest reached beyond the school district, and Craig Sawyer, lawyer for the Iowa Civil Liberties Union, announced that he would represent the students at the school board meeting. Sawyer argued that the school was stifling the students' First Amendment right to free speech and expression. The school board countered that free speech was permissible but not at school, where it could be disruptive and possibly dangerous for the students.

On December 23, spurred into action by protestors like Mary Beth, the U.S. government declared a thirty-hour Christmas truce. Mary Beth and others received many phone calls and letters supporting their right to protest the war and to wear armbands in school.

However, many Americans supported the war and thought that protests were unpatriotic. Unable or unwilling to separate the right to free expression from the war itself, some people were hostile to Mary Beth and her family. They received several mean-spirited calls, including one on Christmas Eve in which the caller threatened to bomb their home. On another day, a woman called Mary Beth and said that she was going to kill her. Someone threw red paint at the Tinker house. Several of Mary Beth's neighbors yelled at her, and a radio talk-show host offered to pay court costs for anyone who used a shotgun against Mary Beth's dad.

Mary Beth returned to school after Christmas without her armband. Christopher Eckhardt said, "We went back to school not because we believed the school board was right but because the school board had the might."[1]

In January 1966, after the school board met again and upheld its ban on armbands, Mary Beth, John, and Christopher Eckhardt filed a complaint in the United States District Court for the Southern District of Iowa. The trial began on July 25, 1966. The court sided with the school district and the case appealed to a higher court, the Eighth Circuit Court of Appeals in St. Louis, Missouri. A three-judge panel heard arguments and ordered a rehearing before the full court of eight judges. In November 1967 the court was split, four to four, thus upholding the lower court ruling.

There was no place for the students to appeal but the highest court in the land. On Tuesday, November 12, 1968, Mary Beth sat with her parents in the front row before the U.S. Supreme Court as oral arguments on case 21 of the October 1968 term, *Tinker v. Des Moines Independent Community School District*, began. After an hour of arguments, the case went under review. There was nothing more to do but wait.

The Supreme Court issued its decision on February 24, 1969, and it took the media by storm. The court ruled, in a 7–2 decision, that students have a constitutional right to express political views, as long as they don't interfere with a school's function. Justice Abe Fortas wrote the court's majority opinion, stating, "[Neither students nor teachers] shed their constitutional rights to freedom of speech or expression at the schoolhouse gate."[2]

When the decision was handed down, Mary Beth was living in St. Louis, where her family had recently relocated. Word quickly spread through the high school, and the new student became an instant celebrity. Mary Beth was delighted with the decision but found her new fame a bit embarrassing.

Mary Beth became a registered nurse and still lives in St. Louis today. She often speaks to students about First Amendment issues. In 2001 the first Mary Beth Tinker Award for the Person Who Most Courageously Defends the Rights of Students was awarded at American University's Washington College of Law in Washington D.C.

Today *Tinker v. Des Moines Independent Community School District* stands as a landmark case in the battle for student rights. Mary Beth challenged public schools' right to punish students for nonviolent expressions of opinion and the Supreme Court agreed with her. Justice Fortas said that difference of opinion, even though it may lead to arguments, is the "basis of our national strength."[3]

"I think through history we've learned that sometimes you have to violate rules and challenge things. You can't always just accept the status quo."
—Mary Beth Tinker

Terry Fox (1958–81)

Heroic Athlete— The Marathon of Hope

Goosebumps danced over Terry's skin as he stepped out of the van and onto the wet pavement. After quickly rubbing his legs and arms to help warm his aching muscles, he took a long deep breath of the cool morning air. Terry suddenly felt a sharp pain in his chest. The ache had been there for several days, but he decided to ignore it. Slowly, he stretched his back and began to walk. As his muscles warmed, he picked up his pace. Today he was determined to make his twenty-six mile goal.

The day wore on, and the sun beat down, heating up the pavement. Terry felt the edge of his artificial leg digging into his skin. The sweat caused it to slip just enough to irritate and rub his stump. Stopping several times to pad the sore spot, he began to wonder if he would make his goal.

Then, from up ahead, he heard the sounds of cheering. Standing along the side of the road were hundreds and hundreds of schoolchildren. With their shouts of encouragement, Terry raced forward. Without stopping, he waved to the children and thanked them for coming out to see him.

As the children's voices faded, Terry's breathing became more and more shallow. Could he make it? Could he go another step?

Terry Fox always loved a challenge. Born in Winnipeg, Canada, in 1958, he was an active teenager who loved sports, especially basketball. With determination and a willingness to practice hard, he won the last spot on his eighth grade team. By tenth grade, he was a starter, and in twelfth grade, he was named athlete of the year. After high school, Simon Fraser University offered him a place on its junior varsity basketball team.

At the end of his first year of college, eighteen-year-old Terry began suffering from pain in his right knee. Four days after he was diagnosed with a rare bone cancer, Terry's doctor amputated the leg, six inches above the knee. On the night before surgery, Terry's high school basketball coach brought him an article from *Runner's World* about an amputee named Dick Traum who ran the New York Marathon. That night, Terry dreamed of one day being able to run again himself.

For the next sixteen months, Terry underwent intense chemotherapy. While in the hospital and during treatment, he marveled at the courage he saw in the other patients, many of whom were children. When his treatments were finally over, he felt lucky to be alive and more determined than ever to run across Canada. He decided to train for his marathon run and raise money for cancer research to help other people like himself. He named his journey the Marathon of Hope.

Terry trained for eighteen months, pushing his wheelchair along sea walls, up steep mountains, and over bumpy logging roads. He pushed until his hands bled. After he was fitted with an artificial leg, he started to run. Running every day for the next 101 days, he trained until his amputated leg was raw.

Finally on April 12, 1980, he was ready to run across Canada. The Marathon of Hope started in St. John's Harbor. Terry ran twenty-six miles a day through Quebec and Ontario. At first, few paid any attention to the marathon, but soon word spread and people began to follow his amazing journey. They watched his unwavering courage and admired his gritty determination.

Corporations began to make donations, some as much as ten thousand dollars. People stood by the road and handed him one hundred-dollar bills. Inspired by Terry's determination, towns across the country held events to raise money for cancer research. Throughout Canada, Terry Fox became a household name.

On September 1, after 143 days and 5,373 miles, Terry stopped running. In Thunder Bay, Ontario, doctors told him that the cancer had spread to his lungs. He flew home and was admitted to the hospital.

On the first Sunday in September, Terry reclined in his hospital bed with a chemotherapy drip hanging overhead. He turned on the television and watched in disbelief: the famous singer John Denver was singing a song just for him. Amazingly, in less than forty-eight hours, the CTV (Canadian Television), network had organized a five-hour prime-time tribute to Terry. Across Canada, millions of viewers watched as the most popular singers of the time paid tribute to Terry's courage and continued his marathon. When it was over, the telethon had raised $10 million for the Marathon of Hope.

As Terry fought for his life, Canada cheered him on. In and out of the hospital, he suffered severe pain and intensive cancer-fighting treatments. For his dedication to raising money and awareness for cancer research, he was named Companion of the Order of Canada, the nation's highest civilian honor. He won the Lou Marsh trophy for outstanding athletic achievement, and donations to the Marathon of Hope continued to pour in, reaching $23.4 million.

One month before his twenty-third birthday, on June 28, 1981, Terry died from the cancer that had dominated his life. All of Canada mourned.

But Terry's story doesn't end there. In September 1981 three hundred thousand people from across Canada ran, walked, or cycled to raise money in Terry's name for cancer research. The first Terry Fox Run raised $3.5 million. British Columbia named one of its Rocky Mountain peaks, just west of Jasper, the Terry Fox Mountain. The Trans-Canada Highway between Thunder Bay and Nipigon was renamed Terry Fox Courage Highway, and in Thunder Bay a statue stands in silent and lasting testimony to the young man's brave fight to help others in need.

In June 2000 the *National Post* named Terry Fox Canada's Greatest Hero. An annual Terry Fox Run is held every September in honor of Terry's courage and determination to help those battling cancer. People from across Canada and around the world participate, continuing Terry's work. Today donations to the Marathon of Hope have reached more than $330 million.

Terry once said, "It's all an attitude, whatever your situation in life. I could be bitter but I can't be that way, because even if I only have two months to live I want to live those two months as best as I can, as healthy as I can, as happy as I can."[1]

The Tradition Continues...

Arn Chorn-Pond (1966–)

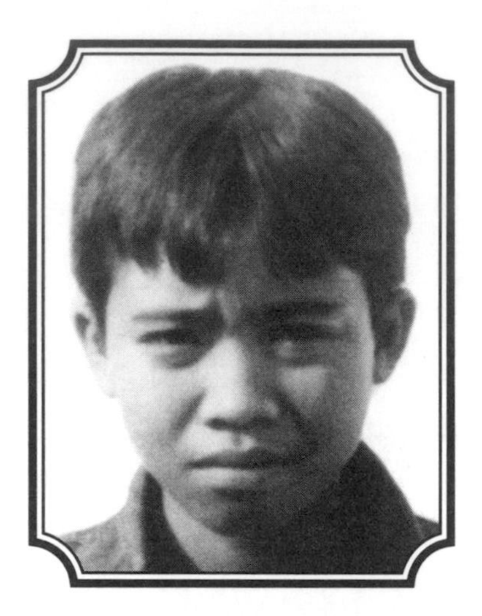

Fighter for Peace in Cambodia

As he lay perfectly still on the cold, hard ground, thirteen-year-old Arn's back ached from carrying his heavy rifle. A child soldier for the Khmer Rouge, each day he was forced to fight for a regime he hated. The Khmer Rouge had taken everything he loved: his parents, his brothers and sisters, his freedom. Arn dreamed only of escape. He had nothing to lose.

Khmer Rouge soldiers were everywhere. They patrolled the area, watching for anyone who tried to escape. But tonight was the night. It didn't matter if they caught him and killed him; he had to get away. If he died, so be it. Death was better than the horror of fighting for the Khmer Rouge.

Arn flipped onto his belly and slid silently across the dirt. He had memorized the area and knew exactly where he was going. Once beyond the patrol area where the other children slept, he ran. The forest floor muffled his footsteps. He ran for hours, deep into the rain forest. As the sun rose, he spotted a dry spot under the canopy of trees.

Taking a deep breath, Arn smiled. It was his first breath on his first day of freedom. It didn't matter if he never saw another person or if he died there in the forest. At least he was free.

Arn Chorn was born sometime in the mid-1960s in Cambodia, a nation torn apart by civil war. His parents ran a traveling opera company, and he was their eleventh child. With too many children to care for, Arn's parents gave him to a childless aunt.

Cambodia is nestled deep in Southeast Asia and borders South Vietnam, Thailand, and Laos. By the time Arn was born, a war was raging between Cambodia's neighbors, South Vietnam and North Vietnam. The conflict between the two Vietnamese countries quickly swelled and sucked Cambodia into their fight.

Backed by North Vietnam, a strong group of Communists called the Khmer Rouge took advantage of the conflict swirling in and around Cambodia and seized control of the government. The Khmer Rouge's comparatively tiny army of about 150,000 brutally subdued a nation of more than seven million people. Led by Pol Pot, the Khmer Rouge immediately evacuated the cities and factories and forced most of the people to move to rural areas to work as farmers. They closed schools, murdered most of the educated population, including teachers, businessmen, and artists, forced everyone to dress in identical pants and shirts, banned all religion, and took over every aspect of the people's lives. The Khmer Rouge was determined to rid the country of any person who didn't fit into its perfectly controlled society.

Arn spent his early days roaming the dirty streets of Battambang, where he lived with his aunt. Arn's father died in a motorcycle accident and seven of his siblings died fighting the Khmer Rouge. By the time the government fell in 1975, his mother had disappeared, presumed killed in a Khmer Rouge death camp.

On the outskirts of Battambang sat the Buddhist temple of Wat Ek. When the brutal Khmer Rouge evacuated all the cities, Arn and hundreds of other children were forced to live and work there. At the age of nine, Arn labored from dawn until dusk, clearing fields and digging canals.

Next to the camp lay a killing field where every day, starting at 6 AM, soldiers murdered men, women, and children. Anyone who said a wrong word or didn't obey orders quickly enough was killed. Sometimes the soldiers killed people simply because they enjoyed it. Each day, three times a day, Arn was forced to watch these executions.

Every day Arn lived in fear. At night, if he slept, the terror of what he had witnessed during the day replayed in his nightmares. Before long, he shut out the world and went into survival mode. Any sign of emotion could get him killed, so he refused to cry. He stuffed his feelings deep down inside. All he allowed himself to think and worry about was food and survival.

One day soldiers came looking for children to learn to play a musical instrument called a *khim*. Arn was one of six offered a chance to escape the hard labor and take lessons from an old music master. As he knelt before the khim in the dimly lit temple, the master begged the children to learn quickly, fearing that the soldiers would kill them if they didn't. The master was right. For five days, Arn tapped the wooden hammers on metal strings, practicing his music, and each day one of the students was taken into the orange groves and beaten to death. On the fifth day, they took away the music master, killing him because he was a teacher.

Only Arn, the best student, and one other boy lived to play for the soldiers. The soldiers demanded that they play constantly to drown out the screams of the people dying on the killing field. The music gave Arn a reason to live and a reason for the soldiers not to kill him. Play and live, one day at a time. In the years that Arn lived at Wat Ek, more than fifteen thousand people were murdered by the forces of the Khmer Rouge.

In 1975 South Vietnam fell to Communist North Vietnam, uniting the two countries into one. When Vietnam invaded Cambodia in 1979, the Khmer Rouge took away thirteen-year-old Arn's khim and replaced it with a gun. Holding a weapon that he didn't even know how to load, Arn faced trained Vietnamese soldiers. Ordered to the front lines of battle and to draw enemy fire, many of the children died during their first skirmishes.

Finally Arn had had enough. On a starless night, he silently slipped into the forest, carrying only his hammock and a rifle. Wearing torn, black Khmer Rouge-issued clothing and no shoes, he ran deep into the rain forest. He ran until he couldn't hear gunfire and the silence became music in his ears.

Happy to be free at last, skinny, starving Arn followed troops of monkeys, eating the food they dropped on the forest floor. At night he slept in his hammock tied between two trees. He wandered the forest for six months, surviving poisonous snakes, starvation, wild animals, and terrible loneliness.

After crossing into Thailand, Arn collapsed in a cornfield, sick and feverish with malaria. The next morning, he was found and carried to the Sakeo Holding Center, a United Nations-sponsored camp for refugees. But the camp was not a safe haven. When aid workers left in the evening,

Khmer Rouge rebels entered the camp and forced some of the refugees to return to Cambodia and fight the Vietnamese.

But Arn was far too sick to go. As he lay on a mat in the area set aside for the dying, a loud voice tore through the tent. "Live! Don't die!"[1] Arn looked up and saw an American minister named Peter Pond looking straight into his eyes. Pond grabbed an IV, hooked Arn up to it, and willed the boy to survive. As Arn recovered, he told Pond about his experiences.

In January 1979 Vietnam overthrew the Khmer Rouge. Nearly 1.7 million people—more than one-fifth of the country's population—died as a result of the war.

The Thai government tried to persuade refugees to return to Cambodia. In response to that effort, Pond and a Buddhist monk named Maha Ghosanando declared the temple inside the camp a religious sanctuary. Thousands flocked to the temple seeking refuge and refused to return to Cambodia. Luckily the Thai government recognized the temple as a holy place and would not violate it, unlike the Khmer Rouge, who would have ignored the sanctity of the religious building.

The Thai military leaders guarding the camp were furious. They arrested Pond and threw him in jail. Fortunately Pond's stepfather was a former ambassador to Thailand and a friend of the royal family. Queen Sirikit intervened and ordered his release. She then offered him three wishes as an apology for his imprisonment. Pond asked permission to take three child refugees back to the United States, and one of them was Arn.

In August 1980 fifteen-year-old Arn traveled from war-torn Southeast Asia to Pond's thirteen-acre farm in New Hampshire. Adjusting to life in the United States wasn't easy. Each night he slept on the floor because he couldn't get used to a bed. He hoarded food, suffered horrible nightmares, and lived in fear of most adults.

Although Arn spoke little English, Pond and his wife enrolled him in White Mountain Regional High School. He struggled to learn English, especially pronouncing the "th" sound, which is absent in the Cambodian language. He strove to understand American culture and to adjust to normal adult authority.

Through all these changes, one thought continued to haunt Arn. Was he truly a victim of the Cambodian genocide or was he partly responsible? Troubled by thoughts of his own actions in Cambodia and the horror of what he had witnessed, Arn felt a deep sense of hurt, fear, and anger.

While battling these demons, Arn threw himself into painting, soccer, volleyball, and music. When the demons surfaced and his anger erupted, his adopted family was there to help. Slowly, with the aid of a counselor and family meetings, Arn aired his feelings and began to share some of his childhood experiences, particularly the death of his sister.

In the security of a loving family and supportive teachers, Arn learned to open his heart, feel, cry, laugh, and love again. In 1982, at age sixteen, he was invited to speak at a peace rally in New York City. He told his story in simple English and touched the hearts of many of the ten thousand listeners. That day, Arn understood that he had power—power to touch people's hearts, power to change attitudes, and power to fight for peace.

A week later, Arn met Judith Thompson, a young woman who worked with Cambodian refugees. Together, they started Children of War, an organization that brings children from war-torn countries together to confront their feelings and speak about their experiences. The first Children of War speaking tour was organized in 1984. It included forty-five children from opposite sides of conflicts like Cambodia and Vietnam, Palestine and Israel, and Protestants and Catholics from Northern Ireland. In twenty-seven cities, these children shared with other victimized children their stories of loneliness, suffering, fear, and hate and even thoughts of suicide.

Arn healed his soul by bravely speaking out about the horrors of war. By sharing his experiences, he helped other children find the courage to survive and gave them an opportunity to band together to end violence and build hope for a better future.

Arn has returned many times to camps along the border of Cambodia to try to help the refugees. During a trip in 1991 he founded Cambodian Volunteers for Community Development, an organization that encourages Cambodia's youth to volunteer in the rebuilding of their nation. In 1996 he founded the Cambodian Master Performers Program, an organization that seeks out and supports the few remaining master musicians and performers who survived the Khmer Rouge. This organization records and documents its performances to preserve and revive ancient cultural traditions that are threatened with extinction.

Arn is the recipient of the Reebok Human Rights Award, the Anne Frank Memorial Award, and the Kohl Foundation International Peace Prize. Today Arn Chorn-Pond is recognized as an international leader in the fight for human rights. He is the director of Youth Programs for the Cambodian Mutual Assistance Association, an organization that helps refugees resettle in the United States. He also works with Cambodian and Latino gang members, helping them find common ground that will end the violence in his hometown of Lowell, Massachusetts. His dedication and love for the people of Cambodia are examples of courage overcoming adversity and of how one person can change the world.

"We [children] are less sure we are absolutely right. Adults who are sure they are absolutely right, they make war over their absolute rightness."[2]

—Arn Chorn-Pond

Ryan White (1971–90)

Fighter for the Rights of Kids with AIDS

Ryan struggled to control his breathing and ignore the pain. For weeks, doctors had poked and prodded his body, trying to find out what was wrong with him. It was the day after Christmas and he was feeling a bit better. Maybe he could go home soon. He was so tired of being in the hospital and tired of needles, hard white pillows, and the acrid smell of antiseptics. All he wanted was his tiny bedroom, his own bed, and for everyone to leave him alone.

Thirteen-year-old Ryan watched as the door to his hospital room slowly inched open and his mother's head popped in. She was immediately followed into the room by his sister, Andrea, and the minister from their church. The looks on their faces told Ryan that something was dreadfully wrong. As the three visitors positioned themselves around his bed, Ryan felt fear grip him.

Holding his hand, Ryan's mom gently broke the news that he had AIDS. The room and everyone in it seemed frozen in time. Questions raced through his head: Was he going to spend the rest of his life in the hospital? Was he going to die?

Ryan White was born a fighter. When Ryan was a newborn, his family learned he had hemophilia, a genetic disease that slows the body's ability to clot blood. But that never stopped Ryan from doing pretty much what he wanted. A self-proclaimed daredevil, he loved hanging from trees and doing wheelies on his bike. These activities were normal for most kids, but they were dangerous for Ryan. If he fell and injured himself, the wound would continue bleeding unless he got medical help. Luckily, within Ryan's lifetime, researchers developed the life-saving drug, Factor VIII. The drug contained blood-clotting proteins that could stop bleeding for people with hemophilia. Whenever Ryan got hurt, his mom would rush him to the hospital for a shot of Factor VIII.

In the early 1980s, doctors discovered a new disease called Acquired Immune Deficiency Syndrome (AIDS). AIDS eventually destroys the body's immune system, making it impossible for the body to defend itself against common illnesses like a cold or the flu. For Ryan and his family, this was scary news. The AIDS virus could be spread through blood products, and Factor VIII was a product derived from human blood. There was no cure for AIDS; everyone who caught it died. Determined to live as normal a life as possible, Ryan decided to keep using Factor VIII and not let hemophilia or the fear of AIDS disrupt his life.

In the fall of 1984 Ryan began suffering from stomach cramps and night sweats. He was relieved when the doctor's diagnosis was hepatitis, a liver infection. But by early December, one day after his thirteenth birthday, Ryan was still gravely ill. After a long and complicated surgery to remove a section of his lung for tests, Ryan learned that he had AIDS.

News of Ryan's diagnosis quickly spread through the tiny community of Kokomo, Indiana, where Ryan lived. At the time, little was known about how AIDS was transmitted, and many people thought that they could catch it like the common cold. In the early days of the disease, even doctors weren't sure how it was spread. Confusion about AIDS led to wild rumors, misinformation, and hysterical panic among many people.

Ryan first noticed a change in the way people treated him at church. Eyes followed him as he walked down the aisle. Heads turned each time he coughed. Adults whispered as they scurried their kids out the door. Someone requested that Ryan sit in the first or last pew of the church so that everyone knew where he was at all times.

Once he was feeling better, Ryan decided to go back to school. He wanted to get up in the morning and catch the bus, study math and history, and eat pizza in the cafeteria with his friends. Though he had hemophilia and AIDS, Ryan wasn't going to stop enjoying life.

Ryan pleaded with his mother to let him go back to school. She agreed, but a few weeks later the school board notified them that Ryan was not welcome to return. Parents were scared that their kids could catch AIDS from Ryan just by being in the same class.

The Indiana health commissioner called the school board and said that Ryan belonged in class. The school board again voted to keep him out. Parents collected hundreds of signatures in support of the school board's decision, promising to sue it if it changed its mind. Fifty teachers also voted to refuse to teach Ryan.

The local television station heard about the school board's decision and reported it on the evening news. By morning, the national news picked up the story. Ryan was the first kid with AIDS to publicly protest being banned from school.

As controversy swirled, Ryan struggled to get on with his life. Finally a hearing officer ruled that Ryan could go back to school. The school board immediately appealed to the State Department of Education but couldn't find a doctor to testify that Ryan was a threat to its students. Knowing that the board might lose its appeal, the principal talked to Ryan's doctor and prepared the students and staff for Ryan's return. Ryan agreed to some extra precautions: skip gym class, use paper plates and plastic forks, drink from a separate water fountain, and use a private toilet.

Hundreds of reporters and demonstrators surrounded the school building on Ryan's first day, which ended as quickly as it had begun. Ryan was summoned to appear in court and face a group of angry and frightened parents who were suing his family, his doctor, and the school for allowing him to return. In the packed courtroom, Ryan listened quietly as parents testified that he was a danger to their children, while doctors argued that he was not. The judge sided with the parents and issued a restraining order. Ryan was banned from the school again.

Fear and misunderstanding about AIDS caused the situation to escalate. Everyone in church shunned Ryan, refusing to shake his hand. Someone let the air out of the tires on the family car, kids biked by and threw garbage on the lawn, and a bullet shattered the front window of his home.

Ryan tried to ignore the threats and focused his attention on talking to reporters, trying to get the message out that you can't catch AIDS through casual contact and that victims of the disease had the right to live normal lives.

In April Ryan appeared in court again. This time the judge took only thirty seconds to overturn the lower court's ruling and dissolve the restraining order. Ryan was immediately free to return to school. But the final weeks of the school year were almost as lonely for Ryan as being at home. Many students were absent and some of the remaining ones taunted him or avoided him altogether.

Things didn't improve when Ryan started high school. By November he was sick and disheartened. He told his mother that he didn't want to die in Kokomo. With money from a movie contract to tell Ryan's story, the family could finally afford to move to the town of Cicero. Ryan vowed never to return to Kokomo.

Cicero welcomed Ryan and with his help, the school launched an AIDS education campaign for the teachers and students. Then it took the campaign into the community. It notified the press, sent speakers into churches, and held public meetings with AIDS experts. When school started in the fall, Ryan was not a threat—he was a hero.

By the age of sixteen, Ryan had a job, a car, and an invitation to testify before the Presidential Commission on AIDS. For the next two years, he talked to groups of students and the media about his disease. By the time he passed away on April 8, 1990, Ryan's courage had given AIDS a human face and encouraged a nation to publicly discuss the disease and search for compassion and understanding of its victims.

Trevor Ferrell (1972–)

Crusader for the Homeless

"There's somebody!" Trevor shouted as the station wagon moved slowly past the street corner. Pulling a pillow and a big yellow blanket with him, he stepped out of the car and onto the curb.

A homeless man, dirty and shoeless, slept on a nearby subway grate. Steam eerily floated overhead as Trevor slowly moved towards the sleeping form. He placed the blanket gently over the man and stepped back, waiting for his reaction. The man sat up and looked at the blanket with a smile of thanks spreading across his face. Trevor grinned and handed him the pillow. A warm feeling rushed through his body as the words "God bless you" followed him back to his father's car.

Trevor and his dad drove around the block and slowly past the homeless man again. Trevor grinned as he watched him examine the blanket, checking out every corner. Then he lay down over the grate and placed the pillow under his head with the blanket tucked around his body and a contented look on his face.

Eleven-year-old Trevor felt that he would burst with joy. How was it possible that such a small gift could bring such happiness? Surely there was a way that he could help more of the people living on the street.

As a toddler growing up in suburban Philadelphia, Trevor Ferrell had difficulty forming his words. When his parents discovered that he had dyslexia, they enrolled him in a private school that catered to kids with special needs. Though Trevor struggled in the classroom, his friends and teachers loved his easygoing, compassionate personality.

One cold December evening, eleven-year-old Trevor flipped through the channels on his television set. Images from a news program caught his attention. He watched as a reporter stood under a streetlight with a ragged and dirty person shivering at his feet. The story was about how the city had declared a state of emergency because the outside temperature was so dangerously cold that people living on the streets would die unless they moved indoors. Every homeless person was encouraged to find a shelter.

Trevor was shocked. Were there really homeless people living on the streets of Philadelphia?

Racing through the house, Trevor quickly found his father and begged him to drive downtown and help the homeless people who were unable to find shelter. At first his father refused, not wanting to drive into the city on such a bitterly cold night. But he finally agreed after Trevor promised to work extra hard in school and finish all his assignments. One trip downtown in exchange for one week of completed homework seemed like a fair deal.

Trevor's father drove the family station wagon the twelve miles into downtown Philadelphia. A quiet but excited Trevor held a blanket and pillow and stared out the window as streetlights and suburban homes gave way to concrete buildings and deserted streets. As his father turned a corner, the darker side of Philadelphia rose up to meet them. Graffiti-covered alleys, boarded-up buildings, and garbage-laden streets spoke of a world far different from Trevor's private school and comfortable home.

The car moved slowly down the street, and suddenly Trevor spotted someone sleeping on a steam grate. His father pulled over to the curb and Trevor got out. He walked over to the sleeping form and gently laid his yellow blanket over it. The man sat up, looking dazed and surprised. Trevor handed him the pillow, turned, and walked back to the car.

The next night, with two more blankets in hand, Trevor convinced his dad to make another trip downtown. Though he was disappointed when the man from the previous evening wasn't sleeping on his grate, he was thrilled when he saw his yellow blanket in the hands of a different person.

He quickly handed out his two blankets but realized that he needed many more to help all the people in need.

Over the next few weeks, Trevor handed out more blankets and extra winter coats. When the family ran out of things to give away, he pulled his red wagon up and down the street, knocking on doors and collecting whatever he could to help his new homeless friends.

It wasn't long before word of Trevor's campaign moved through his neighborhood and into his church. Donations flooded in, filling his garage with blankets, jackets, and food. One day an anonymous person donated a blue Volkswagen van. Now, with the help of volunteers and the new van, Trevor was able to deliver not only blankets and clothing but coffee and sometimes an entire meal as well.

Twenty-one days after Trevor's first venture into the streets of Philadelphia, a local reporter wrote an article about his campaign for the *Main Line Times*. From that article, Philadelphia television news stations, the *New York Times*, and the wire services picked up the story. Within a week, people across the nation were inspired by Trevor's work.

While adults busily praised his efforts, Trevor faced a far more difficult challenge. That fall he entered sixth grade and transferred to Welsh Valley Middle School. Gone were the days of encouraging teachers, longtime friends, and the familiar settings of his private school. He was now the new kid, an unwilling celebrity, and still struggling with his dyslexia. Trevor found friendships hard to come by at his new school.

Many afternoons Trevor would return home from school discouraged. He would quietly go to his room, emerging only when it was time to go downtown. For Trevor, the campaign work filled a lonely spot in his life. When he was on the street with his homeless friends, he felt loved and accepted.

Trevor's single night of handing out blankets blossomed into a citywide campaign for the homeless. Organizing hundreds of volunteers, preparing thousands of meals, and sorting tens of thousands of donated items became a full-time job for Trevor and his family. In addition, Trevor had many talk show appearances, school and church visits, and a twenty-two-city speaking tour to spread his message. In recognition of his good work, Trevor's school principal declared a Trevor Ferrell Day.

As the weeks passed, Trevor learned more and more about life on the streets. He witnessed the shocking side of street life—the mentally ill, the drug addicts, the crime. And he witnessed the kinder side—people thankful for the small things in life like food, blankets, and a smile. All around him he saw tiny acts of kindness making big improvements in lost and forgotten lives.

As Trevor's love for his homeless friends increased, he refused to be discouraged by the enormity of the job. So many people still needed his help. Then another idea started to take shape—a place where his street friends could live. A house. A home. Someplace safe from the dangers of the streets.

In March Trevor pushed open the dark green door of an abandoned building on Poplar Street. Donated by the Peace Mission Movement, the house was a gigantic thirty-three-room, nineteen-bathroom hotel set among overgrown empty lots, rusty discarded cars, and boarded-up storefronts. The building was theirs, free of charge, no strings attached. To Trevor it was a spooky, three-floor, rat-infested mess filled with immense possibility.

Determined to see the old hotel transformed into a haven of hope for the homeless, Trevor and his parents started fixing it up. They named it Trevor's Place, and with volunteer help from carpenters, cleaners, and painters, the building quickly turned into a sanctuary of warmth and security.

Twenty years later, Trevor's Campaign for the Homeless is a nonprofit organization and a leader in supporting the homeless in the Philadelphia area and beyond. Trevor's Next Door opened in 1991 next to Trevor's Place and doubled the number of homeless the Campaign could house. Over the years, Trevor's Campaign has housed more than 1,700 people, raised more than $13 million, and offered more than twenty-five thousand volunteers a chance to help the homeless.

Today Trevor and his family manage Trevor's Thriftshop, a store where the homeless can get the supplies they need to transition into jobs and living on their own. Trevor and his Campaign for the Homeless continue to inspire people across the nation and overseas. One boy, with one blanket and one pillow, opened a door for the homeless, offering them a future filled with hope.

"Trevor, yours is the living spirit of brotherly love . . . Thank you, thank you. You are [a] hero of our hearts. We look at you and know it's true . . . nothing is impossible, no victory is beyond our reach, no glory will ever be too great."
—President Ronald Reagan, State of the Union, 1986

Iqbal Masih (1982–95)

Fighter Against Child Labor

In the eerie light of dawn, ten-year-old Iqbal raced to the factory. Stopping for a moment to catch his breath, he sadly watched as hundreds of children shuffled towards the factory gate.

Silently, he joined the group, knowing exactly how to act. Only a few months earlier he had been a child worker, just like them. Keeping his eyes lowered, he willed his body to relax, to blend in with the other children. Several boys looked at him, but their expressionless faces and sad, lifeless eyes assured Iqbal that they didn't care who he was or what he was doing there.

Suddenly one of the guards raised an arm, stopping the children's forward momentum into the factory. As the guard searched each face, Iqbal mimicked the other children's dull expressions. The guard never noticed him.

Once inside, Iqbal found a place to hide. When the work began and the guards left, he went over to the children. In whispers, he asked them about their treatment. One by one, Iqbal mentally recorded their stories of hunger and abuse. By the end of the day, he knew that he had enough evidence to force a raid on this factory. Soon the hundreds of children working there would be free.

Iqbal Masih was born in 1982 in a two-room hut nestled in the back streets of Muridke, Pakistan. Pakistan is a country of rigid social classes. If you are born poor, it is hard to move into a different social class. Unfortunately for Iqbal, his future was already determined by his poverty and the prejudice and discrimination of an unfair class system.

Pakistan's social system is woven together in a tight web of relationships. A child born into the privileged class could expect an education, a job, and eventually a good marriage. Business transactions, job offers, or marriage proposals were seldom extended to anyone outside one's own societal group. Since Iqbal's family was part of a minority class, he was outside of mainstream society and his destiny was hard labor, disease, hunger, and an early death.

By the age of three, Iqbal was already contributing to the family. His tiny fingers busily planted seeds in the family's small garden. He scrubbed and cleaned the laundry and gleaned grain from the local fields. An energetic boy, he loved to play cricket with his friend Fariq Nadeem and dreamed of one day signing with a professional team. But Iqbal's life changed when his father, Saif Masih, deserted the family. His mother had to go to work while his sister cared for Iqbal and the younger children.

In 1986 Iqbal's older brother decided to marry and his father returned. In Pakistan a wedding celebration is very important and the father is expected to pay for part of the ceremony. But Saif had no money. He approached Arshad, the owner of a carpet factory, and asked for a loan of six hundred rupees (about twelve U.S. dollars). Saif signed a contract and secured the loan by offering Iqbal's labor as collateral.

According to the contract, Iqbal must work in Arshad's carpet factory for the next five years in order to pay off his father's debt. With this simple transaction, Iqbal's childhood ended and he joined the more than eight million other children in similar debt bondage. Of Pakistan's working children, more than one-half died before their twelfth birthday, many from malnutrition, disease, or work-related injuries. Four-year-old Iqbal's future looked bleak.

On his first day of work, Iqbal crawled out of bed at four in the morning. In darkness, he walked to the street where he was picked up by the carpet master and driven two kilometers to the carpet factory. Once there, Iqbal entered a windowless room, lit by two bare lightbulbs. Twenty children busily worked at their looms. For his first year, Iqbal was in training. He received no wages and was chained to his loom so he wouldn't escape. For twelve hours a day, and sometimes more, he squatted on a wooden platform and wove. He received thirty minutes off for lunch and, after the training period, was paid one rupee a day (about three U.S. pennies).

Iqbal's spirit rebelled against the injustice of his fate. No matter how hard he worked, his debt just kept growing. Arshad was free to add the cost of maintaining the looms or buying raw materials to Iqbal's original debt. He could also fine Iqbal for mistakes, laziness, and even lost time due to illness. While crouching by his loom, it slowly dawned on Iqbal that he would never be able to repay what his father owed. By the time that he was ten years old, his debt had grown to thirteen thousand rupees (about 419 U.S. dollars)—more than ten times his father's original debt! Iqbal feared that he would spend the rest of his life in the factory.

It wasn't just the backbreaking labor or the dishonest accounting that angered Iqbal; it was the abuse. When he refused to work overtime, he was beaten. When he accidentally injured his finger with his weaver's tool, hot oil was dripped on the wound so that Iqbal wouldn't bleed onto the fabric. If he became ill or lagged behind, he was locked in a room by himself. Arshad even threatened him with death if he tried to escape.

Iqbal refused to give up on his future. When he was ten, Arshad woke him at home at three in the morning and then dragged him to the factory to repair some rugs. Angry and indignant, Iqbal escaped and ran to the police for help. Standing before an officer, he reported the abuse and Arshad's beatings. To his amazement, the policeman ignored his fresh cuts and bruises and marched him right back to the factory. A sergeant handed Iqbal over to Arshad and presented him with a set of chains to lock Iqbal to his loom.

In September 1992 Iqbal heard about a meeting in the nearby village of Shekhupura. A man named Essan Ulla Khan was going to speak about Pakistan's new child labor laws. The founder of the Bonded Labor Liberation Front (BLLF), Khan was dedicated to freeing Pakistan's twenty million bonded workers who were unable to pay off their debts.

On the day of the meeting, Iqbal worked sixteen hours in almost 120 degree-heat. Even though he was exhausted and dehydrated, he dragged himself to the meeting. There he learned that new laws in Pakistan had declared the bonded labor system illegal, nullifying his debt to Arshad.

After the meeting, Iqbal clung to a copy of the Charter of Freedom and enthusiastically presented it to Arshad. Arshad responded by savagely beating Iqbal, who managed to escape and run home.

Two days later, Arshad appeared at Iqbal's hut, demanding that the boy return to work. Iqbal refused. A frightened Iqbal turned to Kahn for support. Together, they faced Arshad again and threatened him with arrest if he didn't hand over a written declaration agreeing to Iqbal's release.

After six years of working in the carpet factory, Iqbal was finally free and able to go to school. The BLLF had liberated more than thirty thousand adults and children and maintained its own school system to help these workers get an education. Across Pakistan, nearly eleven thousand rescued children attended these schools and lived in protected dormitories. Iqbal absorbed all the knowledge he could and finished a four-year course of study in two years.

While attending school, Iqbal became a valuable ally for Kahn and the BLLF. He traveled around Pakistan, educating people about the new laws and freeing children. In the village of Kasur, Iqbal managed to enter one factory and question the children about their treatment. The evidence he collected led to an investigation and generated so much attention that the police were forced to raid the factory and liberate three hundred malnourished, abused children between the ages of four and ten.

By the time he was twelve, Iqbal was president of the Bonded Child Carpet Workers Association in his hometown of Muridke and president of the BLLF's children's division. He passionately and fearlessly addressed crowds in schools, public squares, and factories. Known throughout India and Pakistan as a child revolutionary, his message encouraged three thousand children to escape their deplorable working conditions and thousands of adult workers to demand better working conditions in their factories.

In December 1994 Iqbal was awarded the Reebok International Human Rights Foundation's Youth-in-Action Award. He planned to use the ten thousand-dollar prize to further his education. He dreamed of attending Brandeis University in Massachusetts, which promised him a four-year scholarship when he finished his studies in Pakistan. He hoped to eventually become a lawyer to help continue the fight for human rights.

Iqbal traveled to the United States to accept his Reebok Award. While there he visited several Boston classrooms. Iqbal spent a day at the Broad Meadows Middle School in Quincy, Massachussetts. His visit and message inspired students to create the Kids' Campaign to Build A School for Iqbal. In the last ten years generations of Broad Meadows students have used the internet to spread Iqbal's story to others. According to the Campaign's Web site, "Over $147,000 has been raised and in partnership with the Pakistani NGO (National Global Network), known as SUDHAAR (a non-govermental organization), many 'Schools for Iqbal' are up and running in Pakistan. For their efforts, the Broad Meadows students received the Reebok International Human Rights Foundation's Youth-in-Action Award, as well as numerous other national and international awards for their relentless [efforts regarding the] Kids' Campaign to Build Schools for Iqbal."

After his trip to the United States Iqbal traveled to Europe and testified before the International Labor Organization. On his return to Pakistan, Iqbal learned that his actions had angered many important people, especially those in Pakistan's carpet industry. It was that anger that may have led to his death.

When Iqbal returned to Pakistan, he threw himself back into his studies and the exhausting work of the BLLF. On Easter Day 1995 he decided to take a break from his work and went home for a short visit. On his way back to the city, he stopped to visit his uncle's family. That evening, Iqbal, a cousin, and a friend jumped on a bicycle and rode to a nearby field to bring Iqbal's uncle his evening meal. As they bumped along the deserted dirt road, one pedaling the bike, one sitting on the back, and Iqbal perched sideways on the crossbars, shots suddenly rang out. A farmworker named Muhammed Ashraf had shot at the boys, killing Iqbal and wounding his friend.

The following day nearly eight hundred mourners attended Iqbal's funeral and burial. One week later three thousand people, many of them children, marched through the streets of Lahore, mourning Iqbal's death and demanding an end to child labor.

Many people assumed that the carpet industry was behind the shooting. Within days, the United States and other countries demanded that Benazir Bhutto, president of Pakistan, launch a thorough and impartial investigation. But the results of the official investigation declared the killing a random act of violence.

Iqbal's death is still shrouded in mystery, but his life and actions inspired many others around the world to take a stand against child labor. In Canada, a young boy named Craig Keilburger started Kids Can Free the Children, an organization that works to free children from poverty and exploitation and teaches them that they have the power to force social change and improve their lives. Another campaign began in Australia, urging carpet retailers to stop selling rugs made in child labor sweatshops. Publicly the Pakistani government finally acknowledged its child labor problems. And on October 10, 1997, United States president Bill Clinton signed a law banning imports made with child labor.

Thanks to Iqbal, millions of children worldwide are free from abuse at the hands of factory owners, but there are still many more who live and work in deplorable conditions. Because of Iqbal's life and message, the fight to ensure a free and happy life for Pakistan's children will go on.

"We have a slogan at school when our children get free. And I request you today to join me in raising that slogan here. I will say we are free, and you will say, free."[1] —Iqbal Masih

Kodjo Djissenou (1977–)

Human Rights Activist

Minutes passed like hours as twelve-year-old Kodjo stood facing the school. Beads of sweat trickled down his temple, winding their way to the corner of his mouth. When he licked his lips, the salty flavor increased his thirst.

The front door of the school opened and the principal walked out. He faced the crowd of students, hands clenched into fists that were pressed against his hips.

"What is going on here?" he shouted. "Each one of you, get back to class or you will be expelled!" No one moved. In silence, the crowd turned to Kodjo, seeking his direction.

Swallowing hard, Kodjo stepped forward while thoughts of his classmate raced through his head. A teacher was abusing her and no one seemed to care. No one would stop it. No one would defend her.

But Kodjo would defend his friend's, and every other girl's, right to be safe in school. It had to stop. And the only way for that to happen was to make the principal listen and take action. Kodjo slowly stepped forward and stood before him. Would this man listen to their demands to stop the abuse? Would he expel all the students or would Kodjo, their leader, be the only one who would be punished?

Kodjo Djissenou was born in the West African nation of Togo, a small country of about five million people nestled between Ghana and Benin. Many people in Togo live in extreme poverty, existing on what they can glean from the land.

Left in the care of an orphanage, Kodjo was lucky compared to many of Togo's children because he could go to school. A smart and fair-minded young man, at age twelve Kodjo learned that a fellow student was being punished for rejecting a teacher's sexual advances. In Togo there are no laws against child abuse and students, especially girls, have little recourse when assaulted by an adult.

Angered, Kodjo brought the issue to the attention of his classmates and organized a protest. They wrote letters to the school, supporting the girl's actions. Led by Kodjo, the students refused to attend classes. The school administration and the police tried to force them to return, but they refused until finally the teacher was disciplined and the national minister of education personally condemned the sexual harassment of female students.

That incident taught Kodjo that there was power in one voice. One person seeing an injustice and standing against it would soon find that others felt the same and would follow his or her lead. For the next few years, Kodjo campaigned to educate Togo's youth about basic human rights—the right to go to school, the right to live without fear, the right to be free to make your own choices.

When he was eighteen, Kodjo founded *La Conscience*, an organization dedicated to educating people and organizing protests that encouraged his country to move towards democracy and human rights. He also started a newspaper that focused on the same issues. The newspaper, also called *La Conscience*, is written and produced by young people.

Like other West African nations, Togo has a child slave trafficking problem. Families living in extreme poverty turn to traffickers, hoping to secure a better future for their children. Unaware that they are dooming their sons and daughters to a life of slavery, parents sell them to a person who promises to train them for a profession or find them a job. Most of the children end up in other countries as slaves.

Through his newspaper, Kodjo created the Rapid Alert Network, a system designed to collect anonymous information about child abuse, child slave trafficking, and missing children. Although Togo's infrastructure is poor,

Kodjo and his staff manage to distribute twenty-five thousand copies of the newspaper to more than half of the country's schools.

In 2001 Kodjo was awarded the Reebok International Human Rights Foundation's Youth-in-Action Award for his outspoken criticism of child abuse and slave trafficking in Togo. Today Kodjo is a journalist who valiantly struggles to educate his people about student sexual harassment and child slave labor. Since Togo still has no laws that protect children from any form of abuse, Kodjo is working to introduce permanent child protection laws. Every day he bravely speaks for those who can't speak for themselves.

"If there is hope for change, it lies with the nation's youth. But before there can be change, we need to teach that there are limits to what is acceptable and that there are better ways to treat each other—without violence." —Kodjo Djissenou

Ibrahim (Alex) Bangura (1983–)

Human Rights Activist

A soft breeze whispered across ten-year-old Alex's face as he glanced down the dusty road. The sun was about to set and the cool air was a welcome relief from a day of soaring temperatures. His destination was still miles ahead. Picking up his pace, he hoped he'd make it to the workshop on time. His stomach growled and a sharp pain twisted in his belly. He hadn't eaten all day and he felt tired and weak.

Despite his exhaustion, he pressed on. There were people waiting for him to arrive to teach his class on human rights. He wasn't about to let them down.

Suddenly he felt a rumble beneath his feet and within seconds he heard the purr of an automobile engine. Looking over his shoulder, Alex saw a jeep slide around a curve in the road and pick up speed. It was racing directly at him!

Alex jumped out of the jeep's path and ran off the road. Moments later, he watched from behind an abandoned car as the jeep skidded to a stop. Alex heard grinding gears as the driver shoved the vehicle into reverse. Dust billowed when the tires grabbed hold of the dirt road and propelled the jeep backwards, towards the spot where Alex had been standing.

Alex's heart raced with fear. He knew that hundreds of kids were kidnapped every day and forced to become slave laborers or fight in the military. Was he next? As Alex crouched behind the car, he wondered if anyone could save him.

Ibrahim Bangura lives in Sierra Leone, one of the poorest countries in Africa. Sierra Leone was torn apart by a civil war that began in 1991 when the Revolutionary United Front (RUF) tried to seize control of the country's diamond mines and then the government. Over the next decade, tens of thousands of people died and more than two million refugees fled to neighboring countries. With the help of United Nations peacekeeping forces, the conflict finally ended on January 18, 2002, when all sides in the war issued a Declaration of the End of the War.

At age ten, Ibrahim, who likes to be called Alex, was desperate for an escape from war and joined PeaceLinks Musical Youth. The organization, which started in 1990, is dedicated to improving the lives of Sierra Leone's children.

A creative and outgoing person, Alex quickly put his talents to work, writing music and skits for the other children to perform. His music focused on how to peacefully solve conflicts, tolerate different opinions, and put the past behind and work for a better future.

Alex's friends recognized his talent and voted to send him to a PeaceLinks conference that taught leadership skills and conflict resolution. When he returned, he began teaching other kids about cooperation and tolerance. He traveled on foot and skipped meals so that he could attend rehearsals, meetings, workshops, and concerts.

Alex also assisted the United Nations International Children's Emergency Fund (UNICEF) in distributing oral rehydration packets during cholera outbreaks, building shelters for homeless families, and working on environmental clean-up projects. Amidst all his other work, Alex focused on helping the thousands of children recruited by the RUF to become soldiers. These children were often beaten, forced to use drugs, and then brainwashed into thinking that it was okay to kill people. Alex's goal was to change their thinking from hate to that of peace and tolerance. He personally helped hundreds of young soldiers to redirect their lives away from violence.

By May 1999 at the Global Hague Appeal for Peace Conference, sixteen-year-old Alex led his band of young people in a performance before international dignitaries like UN Secretary General Kofi Annan. He also taught several workshops at the conference and served as a panel speaker on peace. In November of that year, he received a Global Youth Peace and Tolerance Award for his work.

Today UNICEF lists Sierra Leone as one of the most dangerous countries for a child to live in, but because of people like Alex who regularly speak out on television and radio, advocating peace, tolerance, and reconciliation, there is hope for a better future.

> *"I want international leaders to pay attention to the causes of children worldwide, children suffering from hunger, sickness, and the brutalities of war."* —Ibrahim (Alex) Bangura

Asel Asleh (1983–2000)

Martyr for Peace

He heard the chanting from blocks away: "Down with Israel!" "Allah Akbar [God is the greatest]!" Fourteen-year-old Asel raced to the window and looked down on a chanting crowd of protestors as they moved slowly along the street. His eyes strained to adapt to the light that shifted between the buildings—one moment the crowd was in shade, the next, in blinding sunlight.

The protestors moved slowly past, fists pounding the air. Asel recognized his friends from school, his neighbors, and even a young boy from the mosque. The young men passed, some wearing headbands with "Save Palestine" printed across the fabric. Others carried placards with "We Want Jihad!" printed in bright red paint.

Asel leaned his head against the edge of the window and helplessly watched the scene. Then, to his horror, he heard the sharp ping of bullets dancing off stone. The police were firing their weapons into the crowd! Asel watched, terrified, as the protestors quickly retreated up the street.

With tears trickling down his cheeks, Asel turned away from the window. This wasn't how he wanted to live. There had to be a better way, but what could he do?

Asel Asleh was born in early May 1983 in the Arab village of Arabeh in Galilee. He developed into a bright student with a warm smile. By the time he was a teenager he spoke three languages and loved computers. But his future was clouded by the shadows of hatred and war surrounding the Middle Eastern land in which he lived.

The land of Palestine, known in ancient history as the Land of Canaan, sits on the eastern edge of the Mediterranean Sea. It is one of the most historic places in the world, the birthplace of Judaism and Christianity, and a sacred land to Muslims. That heritage has made it a center of conflict for thousands of years.

In 1920, following World War I, the League of Nations placed Palestine under the control of Great Britain. After World War II, a huge number of Jews immigrated to Palestine, buying land and building settlements, with the hope of establishing a Jewish homeland. The Arabs already living there rejected the idea and fought bitterly with the Jewish populations. In 1947 Britain turned the "Palestinian problem" over to the United Nations. A commission decided to divide the land into two separate areas, one for Jews and one for Arabs. The Jews agreed but the Arabs who lived in the Jewish territory did not. Fighting broke out.

On May 14, 1948, the Jews declared Israel an independent state. The very next day, Arab nations surrounding Israel invaded and three major wars followed. When the fighting finally ended in 1973, Israel held the original territory of Palestine and some territory from Egypt.

Over the next few years, Israel returned the lands that had belonged to Egypt but kept the Arab Gaza Strip, Golan Heights, and the West Bank. Many Arabs in Israel and the occupied territories don't recognize the State of Israel and continue to fight for an independent Palestinian state.

When Asel was fourteen, he grew tired of the violence and hatred that was a way of life for so many of his friends and neighbors. His search for a different path led him to Seeds of Peace, an organization that brings young people together from opposing nations and introduces them to the human faces of those they had been raised to hate.

Asel embraced the Seeds of Peace message and preached peace to anyone who would listen. He believed that it was possible for Israelis and Arabs to live in harmony. In the youth magazine the *Olive Branch*, he wrote, "I can never take the word *Israel* off my passport, or the word *Arab*, which I feel proud of . . . We don't have to be caught [between the two]; we can lead these two worlds."[1]

Asel was a leader and an ideal seed. At a 1998 Swiss summit, fifteen-year-old Asel helped bring Israeli and Palestinian youths together and drafted the Charter of Villars, which called for the sharing of Jerusalem by Israel and Palestine. He contributed articles to the *Olive Branch* and shared his views on Seedsnet, a secure online chat room where teenagers working for peace can keep in contact with each other. He also spoke to high school students. His passionate and persuasive e-mails and speeches convinced both Arabs and Jews to call him friend.

Asel was passionate in his support of the Palestinians and their right to a homeland and independence. Because of that belief, he disapproved of the Israeli occupation but understood that violent riots and protests would never achieve their goal.

On Monday, October 2, 2000, Asel attended his first demonstration, proudly wearing a green Seeds of Peace T-shirt. His family and friends will never understand why this peacemaker chose to be there on that fateful day. When violence broke out, passionate, peace-loving Asel was caught in the crossfire.

Asel's death shook the very foundations of Seeds for Peace and left a gaping hole in the hearts of many Palestinians and Israelis. While Asel's family struggled with its loss, the Arab and Jewish members of Seeds of Peace were faced with the first martyr for their cause. To his Arab friends, Asel was a victim of Israeli racism and unchecked force. To his Jewish friends, his death raised a difficult question: How can I love the man whom others say I must hate?

In memory of Asel, his fellow seeds stand united with an olive branch, the international symbol of peace, firmly protecting their hearts. They promise to carry on the Seeds for Peace motto: To enable people blinded by hatred to see the human faces of their enemies. To equip the next generation with the tools to end the violence and become the leaders of tomorrow.

Asel Asleh will be remembered for his leadership and commitment to the cause of peace in the Middle East. As an Arab-Israeli, he was often caught in the middle of two warring factions but chose to see himself as a bridge, connecting both sides of the conflict. (For more information about Asel Asleh please visit: http://www.slider17.com/)

"We can't change what we are, but we can change the way that we live . . .
We can take our lives in our hands once again, we can move
from a position as a viewer of this game to a player . . .
We can lead these two worlds."[2] —Asel Asleh

Henna Bakshi (1989–)

Recipient of the Geeta Chopra Award for Bravery

Slipping out from under the covers, ten-year-old Henna sat up and planted her feet firmly on the cool, wooden floor. She felt her head ache as a violent shiver trembled through her body. She had been sick for a week and the fever hadn't broken.

The room seemed to sway as she stood and she struggled to keep her balance. Holding on to her bedpost, she closed her eyes and willed her body to cooperate. She had to move; she had to follow the intruder who had entered her bedroom and was now heading down the hallway to her parents' room.

Gathering her strength, she silently moved across the floor, holding on to the dresser and then the doorknob for stability. When she reached the hallway, she saw the intruder leaning over her father. Instantly she knew what she had to do.

As her piercing scream echoed through the house, Henna saw her father open his eyes in alarm. The intruder spun around to stare at her. He raced through the doorway and past Henna. She leaped forward, flinging her body towards his feet. As she landed, she grabbed the man's ankle and hung on.

The intruder dragged her across the floor as he headed towards the front door. Henna closed her eyes and clung to him with all her might. She was terrified that if he got away, he might return and kill her and her family. She was not going to let go.

Henna Bakshi was born in 1989, the oldest girl of a prominent military family. Her father, Army Lieutenant Colonel Pradeep Bakshi, was stationed at the military base in Jodhpur, Rajasthan, in northwestern India. When the military transferred him to Ambala, the family moved, and Henna began attending the Convent of Jesus and Mary school.

During the first week of August 1999, ten-year-old Henna became ill with a serious case of typhoid. Suffering from fever, nausea, and loss of appetite, she dozed during the day and was often wide-awake at night. In the early hours of August 3, Henna was startled by a strange noise. Three intruders were breaking the grill on a drawing room window. One of them crawled inside, moved through the house, and entered Henna's bedroom.

Frightened, she listened as the man quietly latched the bedroom door and shuffled towards her bed. Pretending to be asleep, she carefully watched the tall, thin man make his way to the steel wardrobe next to her bed. For several agonizing minutes, he stared at the wardrobe. Then he tried to open it. Unsuccessful, he turned away, unlatched the bedroom door, and headed out of the room.

Henna silently slipped out from under the covers and followed him to her parents' bedroom. The moment he leaned over her father to see if he was asleep, Henna screamed.

The noise frightened the man and he raced towards the doorway where Henna stood. He shoved her onto the floor as he ran past. Henna immediately jumped up, refusing to let him get away. While her father struggled to understand what was happening, Henna took action. She chased after the intruder, jumped at him, and grabbed his legs. She hung on with all her might as he dragged her towards the main house doors and called out to warn his friends waiting outside. Just when it seemed like she couldn't hold on to him a second longer, her father caught up to them, punched the man in the nose, and overpowered him. The other men heard the commotion and ran away.

Henna and her father held the intruder until police arrived. She later learned that the stranger was the son of a maid who worked at the base. A member of a gang of thieves, he was also responsible for stealing cash and official documents from her house on two other occasions. Henna's courage allowed police to arrest other members of a gang responsible for more than one hundred thefts in her community.

Henna accepted the Geeta Chopra Award, India's highest honor for bravery shown by girls, in August 2001. On August 15 she was awarded the Jeevan Raksha Padak, an award given "for courage and promptitude under circumstances of great danger to the life or bodily injury of the rescuer."[1]

Today Henna still attends the Convent of Jesus and Mary school in Ambala, where she helps collect money and clothing for poor children. When she grows up, she plans to become a fighter pilot in the Indian Air Force.

Mayerly Sanchez (1984–)

Founder of the Colombia Children's Movement for Peace

The ache of unshed tears competed with the pounding in her temples as twelve-year-old Mayerly fell exhausted onto her bed. Afternoon sunlight streamed into the room, spotlighting the dancing dust motes in the air. Mayerly lay, unable to move, unable to cry, unable to feel.

Only two hours earlier, she had joined friends and family in mourning the death of her dear friend Milton. The grief Mayerly witnessed tore at her heart, and as the church service ended, she too broke down and wept. She knew that her tears were a mixture of sorrow and anger—sorrow for the loss of her friend, anger that he had not been more careful, but, most of all, anger at the senseless violence that had claimed the lives of so many young men in her country.

She lay staring at a crack in the ceiling, letting her eyes travel along every curve until the crack disappeared into the shadows of a corner. Every day in Colombia, hundreds of young people were dying. As she closed her eyes, Mayerly whispered, "I will never forget you, Milton. I promise that somehow I will find a way to fight for peace."

Her thoughts kept going around in circles. When will the fighting stop? When will this insanity end?

Mayerly Sanchez lives in Colombia, South America, one of the most violent countries in the world. Colombia's civil war has raged for more than four decades and has claimed hundreds of thousands of lives. The current civil war began in 1960, when left-wing guerillas tried to overthrow the government and form a Marxist state. Since then, liberal guerilla forces and conservative paramilitary forces, both backed by illegal drug lords, have brutally attacked each other, trapping civilians in the crossfire. The Colombian government, in an effort to stop these rebel groups, only adds to the violence that the Colombian people face each day. None of the groups on their own have the military strength or popular support to overthrow the government. As a result, violence and instability pervade the country.

One of the thousands who died as a result of Colombia's internal conflict was fifteen-year-old Milton Piraguata, Mayerly's neighbor and dear friend. Milton was stabbed to death only a few blocks from his home in Soacha, a suburb of Colombia's capital city of Bogota. At his funeral, Mayerly made a promise to Milton that she would work to put an end to the violence in their country. Twelve-year-old Mayerly kept her promise: Later that year she attended a World Vision-sponsored conference and found the support needed to establish the Colombian Children's Movement for Peace.

That same year, Mayerly organized a children's election day. On October 25, 1996, more than 2.7 million children went to the polls and expressed their wishes to see peace in Colombia. "That day, guns everywhere fell silent."[1]

The children's courage to speak out inspired a similar nationwide event for adults. One year later, on October 26, 1997, more than ten million adults, in the largest social mobilization in Colombia's history, went to the polls and symbolically voted "yes" to the Citizen's Mandate for Peace, Life, and Freedom. Although not a politically binding mandate, the vote forced the 1998 presidential campaigns to focus on the issue of peace. When President Andres Pastrana took office in August, he wore a green ribbon, the symbol of the Mandate, on his lapel.

Today Mayerly leads a national Movement for Peace with more than one hundred thousand child activists. These children educate and mobilize other children to seek an end to the violence by holding rallies, media campaigns, art contests, and school projects and by speaking to other children one-on-one.

Word about the children's peace movement spread, and in 1998 Nobel Peace Prize laureate Jose Ramos-Horta nominated the Colombian Children's Movement for Peace and its young leaders for a Noble Peace Prize, marking the first time a nomination went to children rather than adults. The Children's Peace Movement has been nominated twice more since then.

Mayerly and every member of the movement are dedicated to one day seeing Colombia become a beautiful, peaceful land. "Children are fighting to help other children," Mayerly said. "They are working with the government and leaders of the country. The goal is to have a movement with a voice."[2]

"A little group that speaks about peace can be killed, but no one can kill ten million Colombians who speak about peace."[3]—Mayerly Sanchez

Leonora Shiroka (1982–)

Fighter for Peace in the Balkans

The aromas of summertime, newly cut grass, blooming roses, and freshly baked bread greeted fourteen-year-old Leonora as she left the sweetshop. A sense of contentment spread through her body. If only she could start every day with a hot cup of Turkish coffee and cold ice cream! But they were treats she could afford only on special occasions, like today's visit to downtown Prishtina and the Museum of History.

Leonora strolled along the sidewalk, glancing into each of the tiny shops that lined the busy street. The yellow stucco of the museum appeared in the distance, its wrought iron gates open and welcoming.

As she skirted a vegetable stand that sold watermelons, pale yellow pears, and orange squash, Leonora noticed a group of Albanian university students marching along the opposite side of the street. They were protesting the university's policy of speaking only the Serbian language in school and using only textbooks written in Serbian. It was an intense and often violent debate. As the students juggled their signs, carefully written in both Albanian and English, they courted foreign television cameras and newspaper reporters.

Leonora felt little interest in the protest, but she was surprised when a group of policemen appeared out of nowhere and surrounded the students. She watched in fear as the protestors increased their chanting, clearly agitating the police.

A gunshot silenced the crowd and Leonora cried out when she saw one of the female students drop to her knees.

Leonora Shiroka is Albanian, an ethnic minority in war-torn Kosovo, a country that had once been part of Yugoslavia. Leonora's dark hair frames her brown eyes and Mona Lisa smile. Like so many girls her age, she loves to sing, paint, and write. But unlike other girls, she lives in a world that is plagued by intolerance and violence.

The nation of Yugoslavia, a combination of regions with diverse religions and cultures, was formed out of the chaos left by World War I. The new country held together fairly well until Germany invaded it during World War II. The brutal occupation of Yugoslavia by German forces caused old ethnic differences to flare, and civil war erupted. After World War II, Communist dictator Josip Tito reunited Yugoslavia and maintained tight control over all ethnic groups. When Tito died in 1980, the government's control unraveled as demands for independence increased. The Third Balkan War began in 1991 and continues to destroy lives throughout the Balkans today.

When Leonora was fourteen, she searched for a way to combat the ethnic conflict swirling around her. There had to be a way to end the violence that she witnessed each day and that plagued her homeland. In her search, she found the PostPessimists.

The story of the PostPessimists began in 1993 at a United Nations' human rights conference in Austria. Young people from throughout war-torn ex-Yugoslavian countries asked the Norwegian People's Aid for help in organizing a conference designed to meet the specific needs of their region of the world. They called themselves PostPessimists because these teenagers refused to be pessimistic but were not yet ready to be optimistic about obtaining peace in the Balkans.

The PostPessimist movement in Kosovo began in 1995 when two teenagers refused to hate each other. They were fifteen-year-olds Ivan Sekulovic, a Serbian, and Petrit Selimi, an Albanian. With ethnic hatred swirling around them, they gathered their Albanian and Serbian friends in an old house in Prishtina and began to talk about peace. In a country like Kosovo, where Albanian and Serbian children aren't even allowed to attend the same schools because of ethnic hatred, the meetings were groundbreaking.

Leonora, like Ivan and Petrit, wanted peace. She happily joined the PostPessimists of Kosovo. The group elected Leonora as their president when she was only sixteen. Under her leadership, the PostPessimists moved forward and attacked many of the problems facing the youth of Kosovo. Leonora confronted each task that came her way, even when the problems seemed insurmountable.

Kosovo has the youngest population in Europe, with 60 percent of its citizens under the age of twenty-five, but these young people are threatened by high unemployment rates and have few educational opportunities. A pervasive sense of hopelessness makes them vulnerable to organized crime, prostitution, and drug and alcohol abuse.

Leonora and the PostPessimists are determined to fight against ethnic division, prejudice, and hatred. Under her leadership, they organize conferences, seminars, campaigns, and workshops in an effort to break down barriers and teach ways of living together in peace.

For one project called Children to Children, members visit high schools to talk about issues like drug abuse and family problems. Another project called Golden Hands invites children from Dernitza to reading, writing, and storytelling workshops. Both programs are very successful and offer hope to children surrounded by the ravages of war.

In the summer of 1999 Leonora and her group of PostPessimists organized Albanian and Serbian youth of Prishtina to unite and work together to renovate a cultural and sports center they could share. About six hundred children bravely put aside their prejudices towards each other and helped with the project. It was an overwhelming success.

Also in 1999 the PostPessimists of Prishtina won the Wright Dunbar Prize for Social Activism at the Global Youth Peace and Tolerance Awards ceremony for its work in bringing together Albanian and Serbian youths.

In 1995 there were only about one hundred members in the PostPessimists network. Today there are more than one thousand. These members prove that young people from different ethnic backgrounds can peacefully coexist and work together. The new president of the Prishtina, Kosovo, group, Diell Bakalli, said, "What we try to do is overcome the bitter past by doing other work and thinking about a better life for everyone . . . We need to work towards stability in the Balkans so that the conflict we have experienced will not repeat itself."[1]

Although Leonora is no longer the president of the PostPessimists, she remains dedicated to the cause of peace in the Balkans.

"I think we are all heroes if we can work for peace and love in the world."[2]
—Leonora Shiroka

Alexandra Scott (1996–2004)

Champion for a Cancer Cure

The smell of antiseptic was the first thing Alex recognized as she forced her eyes open. The curtains were drawn, shutting out the morning sun. A tiny, red light glowed on the wall, and four-year-old Alex knew that it would flash if she pushed the button and called for her nurse.

Gently shifting onto her side, she saw her mother dozing next to her bed in a brown vinyl chair with a copy of Little House on the Prairie *lying open on her lap. Alex felt safe with her mom in the room. A familiar, loving face was a comfort in this scary, unpredictable place.*

For the past few days, Alex had suffered through another painful cancer treatment that was designed to save her life. The doctors seemed optimistic, but sometimes Alex wondered if she was going to die.

Only the day before, she had asked her doctor why he hadn't found a cure for this disease. His reply surprised her. He said that many smart doctors were working on it. They were coming up with new ideas and new treatments every day, but for now, there wasn't a cure.

Alex wondered why so many smart people, working together, couldn't find a cure for cancer. She decided that the doctors must need help—her help. Somehow she was going to assist them in finding a cure.

Alexandra Scott entered the world on January 18, 1996, and from that moment, she began changing lives. As a newborn, she was a tiny bundle of joy, but over the following months, she turned into a cranky, colicky, and obviously miserable baby. Frightened by the change, her parents sought help from doctors and became frustrated when they couldn't find anything wrong with her. Her low-grade fevers, short bouts of sleep, weight loss and knowing that she was in constant pain, drove them crazy. Something was terribly wrong with Alex.

Shortly before her first birthday, Alex was taken to the hospital, where doctors found a growth on her spine and diagnosed her with neuroblastoma, an often fatal cancer that attacks the nervous system. Doctors began chemotherapy treatments, and baby Alex was in a battle for her life.

By the time Alex was four, her courage, determination, and indomitable spirit were apparent to everyone. With various cancer treatments destroying her immune system, Alex began a long and painful stem cell transplant that would hopefully restore her stem cell counts.

In the midst of her pain, Alex realized that there were many other children facing cancer diagnoses and treatments just as frightening as hers. When she looked around at all the hurting families, her heart cried out and she longed for a way to help. Somehow there had to be a way to fight this terrible disease.

From her hospital bed, Alex decided that if the doctors couldn't find a cure for cancer on their own, then they needed her help. "When I get out of here, I want to have a lemonade stand," she said. "But I don't want to keep the money; I want to give it to my hospital to help them find a cure."

With a firm belief in the importance of her cause, Alex opened her first lemonade stand in July 2000. As she sat in the front yard of her West Hartford, Connecticut, home, she was amazed by the generosity of strangers. The local newspaper had published a short article about her two days earlier and donations were already pouring in through the mail. On the day her stand opened, people from all over Hartford stopped by for a drink. With help from her brother, Patrick, some neighborhood kids, and her parents, Alex raised two thousand dollars in one day! And, as Alex noticed, no one ever asked for change.

Since that first lemonade stand, Alex faithfully held one lemonade sale each year—even after she and her family moved to Philadelphia in 2001 to be near the Children's Hospital of Philadelphia, the number-one ranked children's hospital in the United States.

As news of her efforts spread, corporations and many individuals have donated to her cause. Alex's lemonade stand fund has raised more than $180,000 for cancer research and the charity as a whole has raised more than $750,000. In 2004 more than one hundred lemonade stand fund-raisers were set up in all fifty states, as well as in Canada and France.

Sadly, Alex passed away in August 2004, but her legacy will live on. Her spirit and resolve offered hope to the thousands of children who battle cancer every day. This tiny eight-year-old girl bravely faced her future with a dogged determination to help researchers find the magic bullet that will stop cancer in its tracks. Because of her inspiring hard work and support, one day researchers will find a cure for cancer.

"The money is to be used to research all types of pediatric cancer, not just mine. All kids want their tumors to go away, and it would be selfish to just research neuroblastoma." —Alex Scott

Dilli Chaudary (1970–)

Antislavery Activist

The first thing he heard was a dull thud that sounded like a heavy sack of grain hitting the ground. Then came the groan—a deep, guttural sound that seeped through the cracks in the window and sent fear racing through thirteen-year-old Dilli's body. Someone was out there and something bad was happening.

Dilli peeked through the window but saw nothing, his view blocked by a giant tree. He inched his way cautiously towards the door, grabbed the knob, and turned it slowly. A sliver of moonlight illuminated several figures standing near the road. Three men stood towering over a fourth man who lay helpless on the ground. When he moved, he was viciously kicked in the stomach, and another groan reached Dilli's ears.

Suddenly he realized that the man on the ground was his father.

Slipping out the door, Dilli tucked himself into a crevice in the giant tree and listened. The strangers were telling his father to stop going to school and to stop learning to read and write. They threatened more beatings and trouble for the family unless Dilli's father agreed. As Dilli watched, the men pulled his father to his feet, punched him, and threw him into a shallow ditch.

Sad and angry, Dilli vowed that one day he would get an education. Somehow, no matter what, he would succeed.

Along Nepal's southwestern border with India lives a tribal group known as the Tharu. With almost 1.2 million people, the Tharu claimed the land between the foothills of the Himalayas and the Ganges River known as the Terai, or the plains. For centuries, they tilled the fertile soil and lived in relative isolation from the rest of Nepal.

In the 1960s the government of Nepal began a campaign to eradicate malaria. The Tharu were naturally immune to the frightening disease and enjoyed a peaceful life since the disease kept settlers away from the fertile plains. But once malaria was no longer a threat, the hill people invaded the Terai, forcefully taking over Tharu lands. One of the men who lost his land was Dilli Chaudary's grandfather.

After the settlers invaded, the Tharu people were forced to work as tenant farmers or bonded laborers. Many accepted loans to pay for necessities like food, clothing, medicine, weddings, and funerals. In exchange for the loans, the Tharu worked eighteen to twenty hours a day, 365 days a year, for little or no wages. Once a loan was taken out, low wages and high interest rates quashed any hope of repayment. Bonded labor, also known as debt bondage, enslaved between seventy thousand and one hundred thousand Tharu people.

When Dilli was born in 1970, oppression of the Tharu was increasing. One day, young Dilli watched as his father, a bonded laborer, was beaten for crossing the border into India in an attempt to get an education. That day Dilli decided that he would fight to get his own education. Despite harassment and humiliation, he managed to complete ten grades, finishing the last two through correspondence courses from Bombay, India.

In January 1985 fifteen-year-old Dilli walked door-to-door asking people to join his Dumrigaon Club. Starting with thirty-four dedicated members, Dilli began educating bonded laborers, helping them fight mistreatment from the landlords and teaching them ways to generate their own income by raising rabbits or mushrooms. Within a month, members were teaching literacy classes in local villages, with a blackboard, a pencil, and a notebook for each student. Landlords and local governments tried to force the Tharus to stop going to class, but the Tharus refused to obey.

Dilli was arrested several times and there were threats against him and the organization, but they continued their campaign. Within three years, the organization's numbers increased to 350. By 1989 there were eighty classes in forty villages. In 1991 the Dumrigaon Club changed its name to Backward Society Education (BASE) and began to work for the abolition of bonded labor in Nepal.

Dilli received the Reebok International Human Rights Foundation's Youth-in-Action Award in 1994 and the Anti-Slavery Award from the oldest international human rights organization, Anti-Slavery International, in 2002.

The Nepalese government declared bonded labor illegal in 2000 but failed to create laws to protect the former laborers. As a result, landlords threw families off their land, forcing thousands of people to set up makeshift camps where they were in danger of starvation and disease. BASE provided food and shelter for them and continued to pressure the government to pass laws and fulfill their promise of giving land to former bonded laborers. On February 21, 2002, the government passed a formal law banning bonded labor.

Today Dilli works to ensure that those laws are enforced and that former bonded laborers are registered and given land to tend. Because of Dilli, future generations will live free of the fear of slavery.

"It is . . . our common belief that human beings are born free, they die free, and they should have the right to live free."
—Dilli Chaudary, acceptance speech for 2002 Anti-Slavery Award

Notes

Tom Savage
1. Bial, *The Powhatan*, 33.

2. Fausz, "Middlemen in Peace and War," 50.

3. Bennett-Stiles, "Hostage to the Indians," 11.

Sybil Ludington
1. Dacquino, *Sybil Ludington*, 42.

James Forten
1. Winch, *A Gentleman of Color*, 46.

2. Ibid., 328.

Levi Coffin
1. Nash et al., *The American People*, 292.

2. Coffin, *Reminiscences of Levi Coffin*, 13.

3. Ibid., 712.

4. Coffin, "The Underground Railroad."

5. Coffin, *Reminiscences of Levi Coffin,* 109.

Louis Braille
1. Bickel, *Triumph Over Darkness*, 59.

2. Ibid., 88.

Manjiro Nakahama
1. Kawasumi, "Reconsidering John Manjiro."

Manu (Lakshmibai)
1. Mahasweta, *The Queen of Jhansi*, 21.

2. Ibid., 58.

Susie (Baker) King Taylor
1. The World Book Encyclopedia, s.v. "Lincoln, Abraham."

2. Taylor, *A Black Woman's Civil War Memoirs*, 88.

3. U.S. Constitution Online,"The Emancipation Proclamation."

4. Taylor, 67.

5. Ibid., 133.

6. Ibid., 141.

7. Ibid., 151.

Ebba Lund
1. Goldberger, *The Rescue of the Danish Jews*, 7.

2. Ibid., 681.

3. Ibid., 9.

4. Ibid., 18.

Claudette Colvin
1. Burns, *Daybreak of Freedom*, 6.

2. Rochelle, *Witnesses to Freedom*, 33.

Mary Beth Tinker
1. Johnson, *The Struggle for Student Rights*, 57.

2. Irons, *May It Please the Court*, 243.

3. Russomanno, *Speaking Our Minds*, 6.

Terry Fox
1. Schrivener, *Terry Fox: His Story*, 175.

Arn Chorn-Pond
1. Cox, "Unchained Melody."

2. Pond, *New York Times*, CN5.

Iqbal Masih
1. Berson, *Young Heroes in World History*, 218.

Asel Asleh
1. de Preneuf, "Asel is Gone."

2. Seeds of Peace.

Henna Bakshi
1. Government of India, Ministry of Home Affairs, "Government of India's Annual Report, 2002–2003," 106–107.

Mayerly Sanchez
1. Jun, "Mayerly Sanchez: Saving the World."

2. Ibid.

3. Children's World, *The World's Children's Prize.*

Leonora Shiroka
1. Thomp, "What Works in Building Tolerance," 18.

2. Campagna Kossovo, "Attivita' Rapporti Appendix."

Bibliography

"Abraham Lincoln." *The World Book Encyclopedia.* Chicago: World Book, Inc., 1985.

African American Publications. "Susie King Taylor: 1848–1912." http://www.africanpubs.com (accessed September 25, 2003).

Alex's Lemonade Stand for Pediatric Cancer Research. http://www.alexslemonade.com (accessed January 13, 2004).

Barlow, Lundie W. "Thomas Savage, Carpenter, of the Virginia Eastern Shore." *Virginia Genealogist* (1963): 99–102.

Baroud, Ramzy. "The Story of Asel Asleh." *Arabia.com.* http://www.arabia.com (accessed January 13, 2004).

Bennett, Jeremy. *British Broadcasting and the Danish Resistance Movement 1940–1945: A Study of the Wartime Broadcasts of the B.B.C. Danish Service.* London: Cambridge University Press, 1966.

Bennett-Stiles, Martha, "Hostage to the Indians: Christopher Newport traded his 13-year-old cabin boy to the Indians, and it proved one of the best deals the English made." *Virginia Cavalcade* 12, no.1 (1962): 4–11.

Berson, Robin Kadison. *Young Heroes in World History.* Hartford, CT: Greenwood Press, 1999.

Bial, Richard. *The Powhatan.* New York: Marshall Cavendish, 2002.

Bickel, Lennard. *Triumph Over Darkness: The Life of Louis Braille.* Sydney: Allen & Unwin, 1988.

Boulton, D'Arcy Jonathan Dacre. *The Knights of the Crown: The Monarchical Orders of Knighthood in Later Medieval Europe, 1325–1520.* New York: St. Martin's Press, 1987.

Burns, Stewart, ed. *Daybreak of Freedom: The Montgomery Bus Boycott*. Chapel Hill: University of North Carolina Press, 1997.

Calvarin, Margaret. "Louis Braille, the Innovator: 1809–1852." National Institute of the Young Blind Men. Universite´s Pierre & Marie Curie La Science a Paris. http://www.snv.jussieu.fr/inova/villette2002/act10b.htm (accessed January 6, 2004).

Campagna Kossovo. "Attivita' Rapporti Appendix." http://italy.peacelink.org/kossovo/articles/art_438.html (accessed December 18, 2003).

Carrillo, Pablo, and Karen Homer. "Peacemaking in Colombia: A Nobel Cause." *World Vision Today*, October 13, 1998.

CBS Broadcasting Inc. "Hope by the Cupful." http://www.cbsnews.com/stories/2003/07/21/earlyshow/series/heroes (accessed August 25, 2003).

"Children's Movement for Peace Nominated for Nobel Peace Prize." *World Vision Today* Press Release, October 13, 1998.

Children's World. *The World's Children's Prize for the Rights of the Child.* http://www.childrensworld.org (accessed December 2, 2003).

Chin, Charlie. *China's Bravest Girl: The Legend of Hua Mu Lan*. San Francisco: Children's Book Press, 1993.

Coffin, Levi. *Reminiscences of Levi Coffin, the Reputed President of the Underground Railroad*. New York: Arno Press and the *New York Times*, 1968.

———. "The Underground Railroad: 1850." The National Center for Public Policy Research. http://www.nationalcenter.org/UndergroundRailroad.html (accessed January 5, 2004).

Copsey, Allen. “Lakshmibai, Rani of Jhansi.” The Copseys of West Norfolk. http://www.copsey-family.org/~allenc/lakshmibai/index.html (accessed November 20, 2003).

Cown, Lore. *Children of the Resistance.* New York: Simon & Schuster, 1969.

Cox, Christopher. “Unchained Melody: Rescued by music, Cambodian child soldier travels extraordinary path to America.” *Boston Herald*, June 24, 2002.

Dacquino, V. T. *Sybil Ludington: The Call to Arms.* New York: Purple Mountain Press, 2000.

Darling, Juanita. “From Mouths of Babes: Give Peace a Chance.” *Los Angeles Times*, October 11, 1998.

de Preneuf, Flore. “Asel Is Gone.” *Salon*, October 7, 2000. http://archive.salon.com/news/feature/2000/10/07/asel (accessed January 13, 2004).

Enabling Technologies. “How Braille Began.” http://www.brailler.com/braillehx.htm (accessed January 6, 2004).

Estow, Clara. *Pedro the Cruel of Castile, 1350–1369.* New York: E. J. Brill, 1995.

Evans, Nickole. “1999 Global Youth Peace and Tolerance Award.” http://www.y2kyouth.org/Global/award02.html (accessed December 3, 2003).

Facing History and Ourselves. “Arn Chorn Pond.” http://www.facing.org/facing/fhao2.nsf/survivors/Arn+Chorn+Pond? (accessed December 5, 2003).

Fausz, J. Frederick. “Middlemen in Peace and War: Virginia's Earliest Indian Interpreters, 1608–1632.” *Virginia Magazine of History and Biography* 95, no. 1 (January 1987): 41–64.

Ferrell, Frank, and Janet Ferrell. *Trevor's Place: The Story of the Boy Who Brings Hope to the Homeless.* With Edward Watkin. New York: Harper & Row, 1985.

Glocester, Rev. S. H. "A Discourse Delivered on the Occasion of the Death of Mr. James Forten, Sr. in the Second Presbyterian Church of Colour of the City of Philadelphia, April 17, 1842, Before the Young Men of the Bible Association of Said Church. Philadelphia." Philadelphia: I. Ashmead and Co., 1843.

Goldberger, Leo, ed. *The Rescue of the Danish Jews: Moral Courage Under Stress.* New York: New York University Press, 1987.

Government of India, Ministry of Home Affairs. "Government of India's Annual Report, 2002–2003." http://mha.nic.in/annual-2002-2003/annual_rep.htm (accessed December 16, 2003).

Haas, Eric. "English Youths Formed Cultural Bridge in Early 17th Century." *Virginia Dispatch* (Winter 1994): 4–5.

Harvey, Pharis J. "Iqbal's Death." *Christian Century* 112, no. 18 (May 24, 1995): 557.

———. "Where Children Work: Child Servitude in the Global Economy." *Christian Century* 112, no. 11 (April 5, 1995): 362.

Hockstader, Lee. "Israeli Bullet Ends a Life in Two Worlds." *Washington Post Foreign Service*, October 5, 2000, A01. http://www.washingtonpost.com (accessed January 13, 2004).

Hoose, Phillip. *It's Our World, Too! Stories of Young People Who Are Making a Difference*. New York: Little, Brown & Co., 1993.

Human Rights Watch. "Togo: Borderline Slavery, Child Trafficking in Togo." *Human Rights Watch*, 15, no. 8A (April 2003). http://www.hrw.org /reports/2003/togo0403/ (accessed December 17, 2003).

Independent Online. "Human Rights Award 'Embarrasses' Kenya." http://www.iol.co.za (accessed January 16, 2001).

Indian Child. "Children of Courage." http://www.indianchild.com/henna_bakshi.htm (accessed December 16, 2003).

Indiana Historical Society. "Levi Coffin: President of the Underground Railroad." http://www.indianahistory.org (accessed February 13, 2003).

Irons, Peter, ed. *May It Please the Court: The First Amendment.* New York: The New Press, 1997.

Jewell, Wendy. "Peacemaker Hero: Ibrahim Alex Bangura." *My Hero.* http://myhero.com/hero.asp?hero= Ibrahim (accessed February 17, 2003).

Johnson, Ann Donegan. *The Value of Facing a Challenge: The Story of Terry Fox.* California: Value Communications, Inc., 1983.

Johnson, John W. *The Struggle for Student Rights:* Tinker v. Des Moines *and the 1960s.* St. Lawrence: University Press of Kansas, 1997.

Jun, Lina. "Mayerly Sanchez: Saving the World." *FreshAngles.com.* http://www.freshangles.com (accessed December 2, 2003).

Kaneka, Hisakazu. *Manjiro: The Man Who Discovered America.* Boston: Houghton Mifflin Co., 1956.

Kawasumi, Tetsuo. "Reconsidering John Manjiro." The Manjiro Society. http://www.manjiro.org (accessed October 14, 2003).

Kennedy, Hugh. *Mongols, Huns & Vikings.* London: Cassell & Co., 2002.

Kuklin, Susan. *Iqbal Masih and the Crusaders Against Child Slavery.* New York: Henry Holt and Co., 1998.

Lee, Jeanne M. *The Song of Mu Lan.* Asheville, NC: Front Street, Inc., 1995.

Levine, Ellen. *Darkness Over Denmark: The Danish Resistance and the Rescue of the Jews.* New York: Holiday House, 2000.

———. *Freedom's Children: Young Civil Rights Activists Tell Their Own Stories.* New York: Puffin Books, 1993.

Linehan, Peter. "The Mechanics of Monarchy: Knighting Castile's King, 1332." *History Today* 43, no. 3 (March 1993): 26–32.

Logan, John. *Tom Savage: A Story of Colonial Virginia.* Chicago: Britannica Books, 1962.

Lukeman-Bohrer, Melissa. *Glory, Passion, and Principle.* New York: Simon & Schuster, 2003.

MacDonald, Robert A. "The Worlds of Alfonso the Learned and James the Conquer." The Library of Iberian Resources Online. http://libro.uca.edu/worlds/chapter7.htm (accessed November 4, 2003).

Mahasweta, Devi. *The Queen of Jhansi.* Calcutta: Seagull Books, 2000.

The My Hero Project. "Peacemaker Hero: PostPessimists." *My Hero.* "Peacemaker Hero: PostPessimists." http://myhero.com/hero.asp?hero=post pessimists (accessed December 3, 2003).

Nash, Gary B., Julie Roy Jeffrey, John R. Howe, Peter J. Frederick, Allen F. Davis, and Allan M. Winkler. *The American People: Creating a Nation and a Society.* New York: Harper & Row, 1986.

The National Center for Public Policy Research. "Fugitive Slave Act of 1850, Section 7." http://www.nationalcenter.org/FugitiveSlaveAct.html (accessed January 6, 2004).

Nichols, John. "The Beat." *Nation* 272, no. 18 (May 7, 2001): 8.

O'Callaghan, Joseph F. "The Cortes of Castile-León." The Library of Iberian Resources Online. http://libro.uca.edu/cortes/cortes2.htm (accessed November 4, 2003).

Olson, Tod. "From School to Supreme Court." *Scholastic Update* (September 17, 1993): 19–21.

Payne, Stanley G. "A History of Spain and Portugal." The Library of Iberian Resources Online. http://libro.uca.edu/payne1/payne8.htm (accessed January 2, 2004).

Plummer, Katherine. *The Shogun's Reluctant Ambassadors: Japanese Sea Drifters in the North Pacific.* Portland: Oregon Historical Society Press, 1991.

Pond, Arn Chorn. Untitled. *New York Times*, December 2, 1984, CN5.

Reebok, Ltd. "Reebok Human Rights Award." *Reebok Human Rights Programs.* http://www.reebok.com/x/us/humanrights/text-only/awards/2001.html (accessed December 17, 2003).

Rittner, Carol, and Sondra Myers. *The Courage to Care: Rescuers of Jews During the Holocaust.* New York: New York University Press, 1986.

Roberts, J. A. G. *A Concise History of China.* Cambridge: Harvard University Press, 1999.

Rochelle, Belinda. *Witnesses to Freedom: Young People Who Fought for Civil Rights.* New York: Lodestar Books, 1993.

Russomanno, Joseph. *Speaking Our Minds: Conversations with the People Behind Landmark First Amendment Cases.* Mahwah, NJ: Lawrence Erlbaum Associates, 2002.

Ryan, Timothy. "Iqbal Masih's Life: A Call to Human Rights Vigilance." *Christian Science Monitor* 87, no. 110 (May 3, 1995): 18.

San Souci, Robert D. *Fa Mulan: The Story of a Woman Warrior.* New York: Hyperion Books for Children, 1998.

Sathu, Dr. Prem Nath. "Significance of the Yagneopavit Ceremony." Kashmiri Overseas Association. http://www.koausa.org/Festivals/Yagneopavit/article2.html (accessed November 25, 2003).

Saunders, J. J. *The History of the Mongol Conquests*. Philadelphia: University of Pennsylvania Press, 1971.

Schapiro, Mark. "Children of a Lesser God," *Harper's Bazaar* 129, no. 3413, (April 1996): 204.

Schrivener, Leslie. *Terry Fox: His Story*. Toronto: McClelland and Stewart, 1981.

Scott, Liz. Interview, December 17, 2003.

Seeds of Peace. http://www.seedsofpeace.org (accessed December 3, 2003).

Sheehy, Gail. "A Home for Cambodia's Children." *New York Times*, September 23, 1984.

Steinberg, Lucien. *Not as a Lamb: The Jews Against Hitler*. Farnborough, England: Saxon House, 1974.

Taylor, Susie King. *A Black Woman's Civil War Memoirs: Reminiscences of My Life in Camp with the 33rd U.S. Colored Troops, Late 1st South Carolina Volunteers.* New York: Markus Wiener Publishing, 1988.

The Terry Fox Foundation. "Terry Fox." http://www.terryfoxrun.org (accessed January 6, 2004).

Thomp, Cathryn L. "What Works in Building Tolerance Among Balkan Children and Youth." International Youth Foundation. http://www.iyfnet.org/uploads/WhatWorksinBuilldingTolerance.pdf (accessed January 8, 2004).

United Nations Development Programme. "Youth Post-Conflict Participation Project." *UNDP in Kosovo.* http://www.kosovo.undp.org/Projects/YPCPP/ypcpp.htm (accessed December 18, 2003).

U.S. Constitution Online. "The Emancipation Proclamation." http://www.usconstitution.net (accessed January 5, 2004).

WayNet.org./ "Levi Coffin House." http://www.waynet.org/nonprofit/coffin.htm (accessed January 6, 2003).

White, Ryan, and Ann Marie Cunningham. *Ryan White: My Own Story.* New York: Penguin Putnam, Inc., 1991.

Winch, Julie. *A Gentleman of Color: The Life of James Forten.* Oxford: Oxford University Press, 2002.

Acknowledgements

I want to thank Victoria and Melody for their tireless search for those endless "details" that I so desperately needed; Barbara and Terri for their editing skills as well as their tenacity and determination in keeping me focused; and the Multnomah County Library reference employees for all of their help in locating these amazing kids. Every book is a team effort. *Merci! Gracias! Domo! Danke!*

About the Author

J. M. Bedell spent her childhood daydreaming in hayfields, talking to cows, and finding her heroes between the pages of books. She is a full-time writer of historical fiction and nonfiction for children. She is currently completing her MFA in creative writing from Hamline University in Minnesota. She lives in Portland, Oregon, with her husband, their youngest son, and two Siberian Huskies. *Finding Courage* is J.M.'s first nonfiction book for children. You can visit her website at www.jmbedell.com.

OTHER BOOKS BY BEYOND WORDS:

ARE YOU PART OF GENERATION FIX?

Read real-life stories of Generation Fixers:

- Zachary Ebers, at fourteen, created Breakfast Bonanza and collected more than 5,000 boxes of cereal for food pantries in St. Louis.
- April Mathews, whose family lost their home when she was ten, started a support program for homeless kids called AfterShare Kids.

Across the country, kids just like you are feeding the hungry, caring for the sick, protecting the environment, and fighting for equality! Read all about them in *Generation Fix*.

170 pages, black and white art, $9.95 softcover

GREAT STORIES OF REAL GIRLS WHO MADE HISTORY!

Did you know that:

- Joan of Arc was only seventeen when she led the French troops to victory?
- Cristen Powell started drag racing at sixteen and is now one of the top drag racers in America?

✻ Scholastic & Book of the Month Club Selection ✻
✻ A Troll Book Club Selection ✻

Impress your girlfriends with even more great stories of women heroines with *Girls Who Rocked the World* and *Girls Who Rocked the World 2*. So…how are you going to rock the world?

160 pages, black and white art, $8.95 softcover

HEY BOYS! WHY WAIT FOR SUCCESS?

Did you know:

- Galileo invented the first accurate mechanical clock at the age of eighteen?
- Bill Gates founded his first computer company and invented a machine to solve traffic problems at the age of sixteen?

Boys Who Rocked the World not only shares the stories of boys who have made a difference in the world before the age of twenty but also profiles boys currently preparing to take the world by storm. Are you one of them? The world is waiting to be rocked by you!

160 pages, black and white art, $8.95 softcover

HEY GIRLS!
SPEAK OUT • BE HEARD • BE CREATIVE • GO FOR YOUR DREAMS!

Discover how you can:

- handle grouchy, just plain ornery adults
- avoid life's most embarrassing moments

✻ Scholastic & Book of the Month Club Selection ✻

Girls Know Best celebrates girls' unique voices and wisdom. Thirty-eight girls, ages seven to fifteen, share their advice and activities. Everything you need to know from the people who've been there: girls just like you!

160 pages, black and white collage art, $8.95 softcover

HEY GUYS!
EVERYTHING YOU NEED TO KNOW ACCORDING TO THE "EXPERTS"—GUYS JUST LIKE YOU!

Read about:

- tips on catching frogs, bugs, and other creatures
- being the best big brother

From making comic strips to dealing with girls, *Boys Know It All* is packed with great ideas from thirty-two cool guys that are just like you!

160 pages, black and white collage art, $8.95 softcover

HEY ADVENTURERS!

What's the farthest place you've ever traveled?
Going Places takes you on exciting trips where kids just like you overcome fears, take on new challenges, and eat weird foods…

- Join Pamela Edgeworth as she tries to survive a week of boot camp.
- Venture with Hannah Jackson to an eco-farm in Ecuador.

Going Places will make you curious about traveling outside of your comfort zone.

152 pages, black and white art, $9.95 softcover

SCIENCE IS AWESOME!

Yes, it's okay, even cool and fun to like science. And guess what? Women and girls most definitely have a place in the science world! Read personal accounts and biographies of female scientists like:

- Mary Leakey who helped discover the oldest fossils of man.
- Mae Jemison who teaches engineering and was the first African American in space.

The Ultimate Girls' Guide to Science introduces you to famous women scientists as well as many aspiring girl scientists of today. Quizzes and activities will help you assess your interests and encourage you to follow your dreams in various scientific fields.

144 pages, black and white art, $9.95 softcover

BEYOND WORDS PUBLISHING, INC.

OUR CORPORATE MISSION

Inspire to Integrity

OUR DECLARED VALUES

We give to all of life as life has given us.

We honor all relationships.

Trust and stewardship are integral to fulfilling dreams.

Collaboration is essential to create miracles.

Creativity and aesthetics nourish the soul.

Unlimited thinking is fundamental.

Living your passion is vital.

Joy and humor open our hearts to growth.

It is important to remind ourselves of love.